L A N D

OF THE

RED SOIL

**A POPULAR HISTORY OF
PRINCE EDWARD ISLAND**

L A N D

OF THE

RED SOIL

DOUGLAS BALDWIN

RAGWEED PRESS
1990

Cover Photo: John Sylvester
Editors: Laurie Brinklow and Catherine Matthews
Design: Catherine Matthews
Printing: Les Éditions Marquis Ltée.

*With thanks to The Canada Council
for its generous support.*

Ragweed Press
P.O. Box 2023
Charlottetown, Prince Edward Island
Canada C1A 7N7

Distributed by:
University of Toronto Press
5201 Dufferin Street
Downsview, Ontario
Canada M3H 5T8

Canadian Cataloguing in Publication Data

Baldwin, Douglas, 1944-
Land of the red soil

Includes bibliographical references.
ISBN 0-920304-96-6

1. Prince Edward Island — History. I. Title.

FC2611.B35 1990   971.7   C90-097563-6
F1048.B35 1990

*This book is dedicated to Gramps
and my parents,
to whom I owe so much.*

CONTENTS

PREFACE

In 1985 I wrote *Abegweit: Land of the Red Soil*. Although it was intended as a grade six Social Studies textbook, the general public seemed eager to read it. Some teachers had difficulty convincing their students to bring *Abegweit* to school because the pupils' parents wished to read it at home. In one school, not a single student returned this textbook at the end of the year. It was apparently cheaper to pay for the loss of the text than to buy a paperback copy in the bookstore. In fact, the thousand paperback copies were quickly sold and *Abegweit* is now out of print.

The phenomenal success of *Abegweit* illustrated the need for a general history of Prince Edward Island. This book seeks to retain those elements of the textbook which made it so popular, while upgrading the reading level and content (all mention of alcohol, for example, was excluded from the school textbook), and adding information from more recently published works.

I relied a great deal on the expertise of Harry Holman and Dr. Thomas Spira in writing this book. Harry, the Provincial Archivist of Prince Edward Island, read approximately two-thirds of the book and provided invaluable advice on content, interpretation and possible visuals for the text. He will not agree with everything I have written, but his comments have made this a much better history. Tom Spira, history professor at the University of Prince Edward Island, loves to edit. I would send him fifty pages to read, and two days later the material would be returned with suggestions for better phraseology, word selections, or noting that I used "programme" and "program", for example, at different points in the manuscript. Acadia University professor Jim Snowdon provided me with the benefit of his expertise on Canada's early history.

Phil O'Neill furnished information on Island bicycling at the turn of the century. Ken Shelton, Deirdre Kessler, Georges Arseneault, J.T. "Mickey" Place, Ruth Freeman, David Weale, F.W.P. Bolger, Harold McGee Jr., David Keenlyside, Nicolas de Jong, Harry Baglole, Jim Hornby and Eldon Jamieson all assisted in the writing of the original text. Laurie Brinklow pursued the idea of writing a popular history of the Island and convinced me to do it, and Catherine Matthews put it all together. The shortcomings are, naturally, mine alone.

Douglas Baldwin
History Department
Acadia University
May 1990

SOURCES

The illustrations in this book are reproduced from *Abegweit: Land of the Red Soil*, © Ragweed Press, 1985, with the exception of the "Debki Dancers" (p.163), courtesy Michael Rashed. The following list defines abbreviations commonly used in captions throughout *Land of the Red Soil: A Popular History of Prince Edward Island.*

CCAGM	Confederation Centre Art Gallery and Museum
HC/CCAGM	From the Harris Collection, Confederation Centre Art Gallery and Museum
PAC	Public Archives of Canada
PC,Hfx	Parks Canada, Halifax
PEIDOT	Prince Edward Island Department of Tourism
PEIMHF	Prince Edward Island Museum and Heritage Foundation
PEIPA	Prince Edward Island Public Archives
PP	Parks and People
TIM	*The Island Magazine*

ONE

Richard Furlong

WELCOME HOME

Welcome home!" Whether you are a native Islander, or it is your first visit to Prince Edward Island, this is the invariable greeting. To all Islanders, no matter where they live, the Island is home. Here they are surrounded by hundreds of uncles, nephews, nieces and other relatives.

Prince Edward Island is known simply as *The Island*, as if it were the only island in the world. The Micmac called it *Minegoo*, which means "The Island", or more romantically, *Abegweit*—"cradled on the waves". Lucy Maud Montgomery, the famous author of the "Anne of Green Gables" children's stories, wrote in 1891: "He said he was from 'the island!' What island, queried a listener? 'What island?' repeated our honest countryman, in amazement. 'Why, Prince Edward Island, man! What other Island is there?'"

Those people unfortunate enough not to have been born on P.E.I. are from "off-Island", or more commonly, "from away". Last names are often accurate clues that a person is not Island-born. The white pages in the telephone book, all 228 pages, list page after page of Mcs, Macs, Gallants and Arsenaults, but contain only a smattering of non-Celtic, English, or non-French names. With eighty-one per cent of its population of British origin and fourteen per cent of French descent, P.E.I. is the most homogeneous Canadian province. Islanders distinguish families with the same last name by their geographical location. "Oh, you're one of the Souris MacDonalds," an acquaintance might say to identify a new friend.

Islanders are proud of their heritage, as the large number of local history books attest. A weekly radio program regales listeners with stories from the Island's past. The people cherish their history, and are proud of their present. They do not wish to live anywhere else, nor do they generally relish the idea of sampling other locales. Indeed, the Island is a good place in which to live. Violent crimes are uncommon, and drug dealers are a rarity. There is no place to hide on a small island where everyone knows everyone else's business— or so it often seems—and the long ferry wait makes escape almost impossible.

Prince Edward Island politics reflect the narrow confines of the Island. The provincial legislature is smaller than either the Montreal or Toronto city councils. Local political meetings are well-attended, and the province traditionally has one of the highest proportions of voter turnout in the country. Political issues are often dominated by discussions over patronage, and most people feel a personal connection to either the Liberal, N.D.P. or Conservative party.

P.E.I. is a crescent-shaped island of red sand, rolling green fields, neat rural settlements, pretty fishing villages and patchwork farms. It is 224 km in length, and from 6 to 64 km in width—comparable in size to the state of Delaware, or with Trinidad and Tobago. No one is more than a half-hour drive from the sea. The highest point above sea level is at Springton (130 metres). The climate is temperate, and few days are completely breezeless. Although the Island is buffeted by a large number of snowstorms, whipped by strong winds, the snow usually melts quickly. Because it is an island, P.E.I. has a milder and more frost-free days than many other places in the Maritimes. Since the beginning of settlement on Prince Edward Island almost four hundred years ago, the Island has often been viewed as one huge farm, and has been called the "Million Acre Farm". The famous red topsoil is not very deep, but it is generally excellent for growing potatoes. In addition to table potatoes, Island potatoes are used for french fries and potato chips, and are exported around the world as seed potatoes.

Fishing is the backbone of many Island communities, especially in Prince County. In addition to providing the major employment for approximately one-sixth of the population, fishing generates additional secondary employment in boat building, fish processing, and

The Riverdale Hills PEIDOT

in the manufacture of traps and fishing gear. More recently, the scientific culturing of mussels, oysters, soft-shell clams and trout have made aquaculture a booming business. However, as the chart reveals, lobster fishing is the mainstay of the Island's fishing industry.

Before farming and fishing, tourism infuses the most money into the Island economy. By 1900, the Island was becoming recognized as an ideal vacationland by travellers attracted by Prince Edward Island's scenery, beaches, and what many people consider "rural charm". Several families built large summer homes, such as Dalvay-by-the-Sea, which now serves as a hotel in the National Park. This park, stretched across the Island's north shore, was established in 1937 to protect such historic sites as the literary home of Green Gables, and to preserve the area's beaches for recreational use. Tourism flourished in the 1950s and 1960s when people had more leisure time and money to travel. In the summer of 1989, over 700,000 visitors came to the Island. This was almost six times the Island's total population. The red soil, green fields and blue ocean offer a panorama of beautiful scenic contrasts. Many people enjoy the one-hour ferry ride across the Northumberland Strait. Vacationers find the warm beaches very attractive, and the National Park on the north shore is second in popularity only to Banff National Park in Alberta. Tourists find P.E.I. a friendly place, and come to relax and forget the troubles of big-city living.

Ample recreational diversity is provided by eleven golf courses; thirty-one provincial parks; tuna fishing; horse racing; Old Home Week in Charlottetown; the Anne of Green Gables farmhouse at Cavendish; tuna fishing; *Festival Acadien*; the Lobster Carnival in Summerside; lobster suppers; handicrafts; the resort areas at Brudenell, Mill River and elsewhere; and the plays at the Confederation Centre. The play Anne of Green Gables has been performed at the Confederation Centre of the Arts every summer for over twenty years.

The beautiful white sand beaches that surround the Island are popular attractions. Compared to such places as Toronto Island, Acapulco and Atlantic City, the beaches are virtually deserted. On some it is possible to walk for miles without seeing another person. The gentle waves and the gradual drop-off make many areas safe for non-swimmers. Sand bars, sea stacks, ever-changing sand dunes and sand spits provide visual variety. Close observation reveals that the shore is teeming with life. Periwinkles, sand hoppers, mussels, several types of clams, crabs, Irish moss, jellyfish, blue herons and gulls are common sights. With a little perseverance, the variety of shellfish can provide a delicious light snack. Farther back in the sand dunes and wetlands are black ducks, bitterns, foxes, muskrat and cranberries.

Capital	Charlottetown (pop. 15,800)
Entered Confederation	1873
Population 1990	130,100 (0.5% of Canada)
Time Zone	Atlantic (1 hour ahead of Toronto)
Provincial Bird	Bluejay
Provincial Flower	Lady Slipper Orchid
Provincial Tree	Red Oak
Senators	Four
Members of Parliament	Four
Provincial Motto	Parva Sub Ingenti
	(the small under the protection of the great)
Big Game Fish	Giant Bluefin Tuna
Urban Area	38% 5660 sq km (0.1% of Canada)
Languages	English 94%, French 4%
Average July Temperature	18.8 C
Average January Temperature	-6.7 C

TWO

P. John Burden

THE FIRST ISLANDERS

A MICMAC LEGEND

A long time ago, the Great Spirit who lived in the Happy Hunting Grounds created the universe and all life. The Wise One enjoyed his creation in the twinkling lights of thousands of stars, the sun and the many galaxies in the universe.

After creating the universe, the Great Spirit sat down to rest. Then he created Glooscap and gave him special spiritual and physical powers. He called Glooscap to share the sacred pipe and said, "Glooscap, I am going to create people in my own image. I will call them Micmac."

The Great Spirit was pleased with this creation. He took out his sacred pipe and again called Glooscap. As the Great Spirit was smoking he noticed a large amount of dark red clay left over. "Glooscap, look at this large piece of clay, the same colour as my Micmac people. I will shape this clay into a crescent form and it will be the most beautiful of all places on Mother Earth. It will become the home of my Micmac people."

The great spirit fashioned an enchanting island and called it Minegoo. He dressed her dark red skin with green grass and lush forests of many different kinds of trees, and sprinkled her with many brightly coloured flowers. Her forest floors were like deep soft carpets which would cushion the moccasined feet of the Micmac people.

Minegoo was so beautiful that it made the great Spirit extremely happy—so happy that he thought about placing Minegoo among the stars. After considering this for a short time, the Wise One decided that Minegoo should be placed in the middle of the singing waters, now known as the Gulf of St. Lawrence.

John Joe Sark
Micmac Legends Of Prince Edward Island
Ragweed Press, 1988, p. 6

This Micmac creation story parallels the Christian allegory in Genesis. Both tales depict the all-mighty ruler as a male, and place humans on the land upon its creation. Scientists from several different disciplines, however, have established that Prince Edward Island was slowly fashioned over centuries. Only comparatively recently has it been inhabited by humans. In fact, if the history of the universe was compressed into a one-year period, humans would only appear on the very last day of the year.

What is now Atlantic Canada appeared quite different three hundred million years ago. Prince Edward Island and the Northumberland Strait did not exist. New Brunswick, Nova Scotia and Quebec were very mountainous. Rivers flowed from these mountains down into the large lowland region, and emptied into the present-day Gulf of St. Lawrence. When the streams slowed down on the flatter ground they deposited small particles of rock, silt and clay. As millions of years passed, layers of these particles, called sediments, created a low-lying plain. When the water in the Gulf of St. Lawrence rose, an island appeared.

The weight of the upper layers of rock compressed the lower sediments into sedimentary rock. Small amounts of iron in the sediments rusted on contact with water and air and left a red iron oxide stain on the surrounding particles. This explains why the Island's soil is red.

For millions of years the Island enjoyed a mild climate. In the last one or two million years, however, the climate turned cold. The snow did not melt in the summer, and as it became thicker, its own immense weight compressed the snow into ice. In some areas in western Prince Edward Island, the ice was one thousand metres deep. These heavy glaciers actually depressed the land below sea level.

GLACIERS

The glaciers of the last ice age began melting about eighteen thousand years ago. As the ice melted, the sea level rose higher than it is today. Parts of Prince Edward Island became flooded and the land was divided into the three separate islands. Once the weight of the glacier was gone, the land slowly rebounded. As the sea level fell to almost forty metres below its present height, the Northumberland Strait disappeared (between eleven thousand and six thousand years ago) and the "Island" became part of the mainland. Later, the water

TIMELINE

Earth is formed	4.5 billion BP
Age of dinosaurs	200–100 million BP
Homo Erectus	1 million BP
Neanderthal man in Europe	100 thousand BP
Alaskan land bridge formed	40 thousand BP
Paleo-Indians	30,000–10,000 BP
Last ice age begins to recede	18,000 BP
Island divided into three	18,000 BP
Niagara Falls formed	13,000 BP
Island joined to mainland	11,000–6,000 BP
Alaskan land bridge flooded	8,000 BP
Stonehenge and pyramids	3,000 BP

(BP stands for "before the present," which by common agreement began in 1950.)

began to rise once again. About three thousand years ago the Island became separated from the mainland once more.

As the glaciers melted, they left a covering of broken rock, gravel, sand, silt and clay. Large boulders, originally from the mainland, were carried by the glaciers and dropped in the west end of the Island near Poplar Grove and Kildare River. These boulders, called erratics, are composed of different material than local rocks. The first plants to grow after the ground thawed were lichens and mosses. They eventually died, decayed, became humus, and helped support additional plant life. The dying plants mixed with the clay, sand and silt to form the Island's topsoil. Partly because the glacial deposits were acidic, Island soil also became acidic and is deficient in natural fertility. (Adding lime is one of the best means of improving the soil.)

The only records of the Island's prehistoric plants and animals exist in the small fossils which occasionally are found along the beaches. Recent discoveries in Nova Scotia suggest that large mastodons inhabited this area of the world between ten thousand and seventy thousand years ago. Perhaps the most fascinating discovery was made near French River in 1845. In that year, in the process of digging a well, several men uncovered the fossil of a *Bathygnathus borealis* that had been alive about two hundred and eighty million years ago. This reptile in the Pelycosaur family was about two metres long, and sported a large fin or "sail" on its back.

EARLY PEOPLES

What we know about early Island peoples has been pieced together from Indian legends, accounts written by European missionaries, explorers and fur traders, and archaeological explorations. Archaeologists examine weapon points, tools and pottery fragments to interpret the past. Geologists use glacier spoors to identify when and where the glaciers existed. Physicists measure the amount of carbon-14 in once-living matter to determine its age. Botanists analyze pollen traces to date campsites and describe ancient vegetation cycles. And climatologists plot the weather through the centuries.

One problem in discussing early Micmac life is accurately interpreting the written evidence left by explorers, fur traders and missionaries. These people judged the natives according to their own cultural standards. Fur traders in search of beaver pelts, for example, believed that natives who didn't actively pursue these animals were lazy. Priests, unfamiliar with Indian beliefs, decided that the natives had no religion. In need of money from France, the Jesuits exaggerated the "savage" nature of the natives in order to emphasize the difficulty of their task. Current concerns also influence how people interpret the past. Micmac and government researchers concerned with Indian land claims, for example, often turn to the past for supporting arguments.

Human occupation of the Maritimes probably began about 10,600 years ago (8,600 BC). Archaeologists refer to these peoples, who employed a unique style of spear point, as the Paleo-Indians. At this time, the Island was still joined to the mainland, the climate was much colder than it is today, and the vegetation was sparser. Mastodons may have inhabited the area, but more likely the Paleo-Indians hunted caribou, arctic fox and hares. These peoples had probably migrated from the New England region after the glaciers had receded. Those groups which lived near the coastline took advantage of the variety of fish and birds which frequented the area. Spears used to kill caribou could also catch seals and walrus. Archaeologists, however, debate whether shellfish was also a part of their diet. Unfortunately, we do not know what language they spoke, what tools they employed, or how many of them existed.

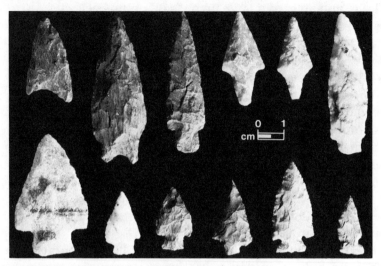

Stone projectile points discovered on P.E.I.
D. Keenlyside (National Museum Of Man)

Equally frustrating is the fact that we do not yet know what happened to them.

From about 9,000 to 3,500 years ago, peoples with a slightly different lifestyle inhabited the Maritimes. This period, called the Maritime Archaic age, was more sea-oriented. Archaeological explorations have discovered a well-developed culture, replete with delicately carved bone and stone figures of birds, killer whales, whistles and hair combs. As the population expanded, the Maritime Archaic people built homes as large as one hundred metres in length, and divided them into separate family units. These peoples may have been descendants of the Paleo-Indians, or they might have been a different group of natives who had migrated northward into the new forests of coniferous and hardwood trees which took root as the climate warmed. Approximately 10,000 years ago, for example, spruce and birch predominated; 3,000 years later, the forests consisted of pine, oak and birch; and by the time the Vikings arrived around 1000 A.D., the land was covered by birch, hemlock, pine, fir, maple and spruce.

Unfortunately, the submerged coastlines have obliterated the remains of many campsites. Because Island sandstone is a soft rock, it is easily eroded by ice, wave and wind action. This erosion, combined with a gradually rising sea level, means that every year the coastline recedes from several centimetres to a few metres, depending upon location. Measurements taken at North Lake between 1935 and 1972 revealed that the cliffs eroded at an annual rate of 67 centimetres. During the last century, as the sea level continued to rise, and the bulge in the earth's crust subsided, the Maritime provinces submerged by almost thirty centimetres, giving rise to predictions of future calamities. Since the natives preferred to be near the water because of its store of wildlife, many of their campsites are now probably under water. Similar to their predecessors, the Maritime Archaic peoples apparently disappeared without a trace.

THE MICMAC

When the first Europeans arrived in the Maritimes there were about eighteen thousand native people in the area. The Micmac occupied Nova Scotia, Prince Edward Island and eastern New Brunswick. The Micmac probably did not develop permanent settlements on the Island, but assembled here in the summer to fish, to hunt for water fowl, seals and small whales, and to gather shellfish and periwinkles. Archaeologists have discovered Micmac sites in the Malpeque and Rustico Bay areas, Savage Harbour and the North and South Lakes region. The area between Souris and East Point seems to have held special attraction for the Micmac. Many of the existing remnants of Micmac life were discovered in *shell middens*. These heaps of sea shells discarded by the Micmac changed the chemical composition of the soil and preserved bones and other organic matter, which the Island's acidic soil would otherwise have destroyed.

Although the natives used local stones found on the beaches, the best materials for fashioning tools, knives and arrow heads existed on the mainland; the Micmac must have canoed there frequently. These vessels measured up to eight metres in length and were fashioned out of birch and cedar. Spruce gum, first chewed by the women and girls to make it pliable, and then boiled with fat, was used to waterproof canoes. The Micmac were skilled woodworkers. They made ingeniously constructed wooden cradleboards which rested on the mother's back supported by a strap across her forehead. This left the mother's arms free for work and protected the child from tree branches. Inside the wigwam the cradleboard was propped up so the infant could see its surroundings. With similar ingenuity, the Micmac also crafted spears, bows and arrows, traps, axes, canoes, snowshoes, fish weirs and toboggans.

Just as our homes differ, Micmac wigwams varied in size and shape, depending upon individual preference and family size. In the summer, woven reed or grass mats covered the wigwams. During dry weather the reeds shrank and allowed more air to flow through the mats, thus keeping the interior cool and smoke-free. When it rained, the reeds swelled and the wigwam became watertight. Animal hides kept the homes warm and cozy in the winter.

Since the wigwams had no separate rooms, the Micmac devised rules to ensure individual privacy. Each family member was assigned a special place in the wigwam. The parents slept at the back. The youngest children were next to their parents—girls on one side, boys on the other. The older children spent the night near the entrance, which would have been the draftiest and busiest section in the dwelling. When a person sat next to the fireplace, it meant that he or she wanted to talk and be sociable. Sitting against the wall, however, indicated a desire to be left alone. The Micmac enjoyed singing and dancing, and organized frequent feasts. Adults played a game with a ball stuffed with animal hair and grass. Teammates tossed the ball back and forth, seeking to touch it against their opponent's post at the opposite end of the playing field. A gambling game called *waltes* was popular with all ages and sexes. It involved tossing six two-sided discs, not unlike dice, into a shallow bowl. Points were scored depending upon whether the light or dark side faced upwards. The discs were made of stone, bone or pottery, and were often handsomely decorated. Small sticks were used to keep score. The Micmac also played a pin-and-bone game, in which a string with several hollow bones attached to it was tossed in the air. The player tried to spear the bones with a stick joined to the other end of the string.

Music and dancing were popular at feasts. Instruments included bone flutes, rolled birch bark and rattles made of fish skins and filled with gravel. Storytelling played an important role as well. In addition to providing amusement, the tales passed on the tribe's history and cultural beliefs to future generations.

Several times each summer, nearby villages met for special occasions. Here, young men and women courted, and the adults arranged hunting boundaries and planned raids on enemy villages. Although each village had civil and religious leaders, all Micmac were free to decide for themselves whether to accede to their leader's decisions. Micmac were never forced to do anything against their will; customs and peer pressures ensured an orderly society.

The most important activity, of course, was earning a living—which meant hunting, trapping, fishing and gathering roots and berries. To catch beavers in the winter, hunters cut ice holes in the beaver pond with a stone chisel, and stood quietly nearby waiting to harpoon or spear the beavers as they emerged from the holes. Another technique involved cutting a hole in a beaver lodge and clubbing the hibernating rodents before they could escape. Moose were hunted on snowshoes. The larger the animal a male caught, the greater his reputation. During the summer, the Micmac relied on aquatic life for sustenance.

The women did the cooking, mending and sewing. They placed red-hot stones from the fire into large wooden cooking kettles. When the water boiled, the women added meat, fish or shellfish. Additional heated rocks were added when necessary. Meat was roasted on a spit. The women used stone hammers to crush seal and moose bones. The pulp was boiled, and as the fat rose to the surface it was skimmed off into a bark container to harden. This solid fat provided nutritious food on long journeys. Hot fat was considered a delicious beverage. Animal fat and bird eggs made excellent paints with which the Micmac decorated their bodies and painted their clothes, wigwams, tools, bowls and ornaments.

The Micmac had a special relationship with nature. The woods and fields were an extension of themselves. The natives were so close to the animals they hunted that they could imitate their sounds, and hunters were often named after the animals they had slain. In the Micmac world, every object had a spirit. Humans were not considered superior to animals; they were equal partners with animals and plants, the sun, the wind and the rain. The hunter would thus apologize to an animal for taking its life. And the dead animal's carcass was treated with respect and handled according to prescribed rituals, lest its spirit warn its fellows to leave the area. According to legend, Glooscap told the Micmac: "If you have to kill a deer so that you can live, you should tell the deer that his beauty will live on to glorify the Great Spirit in the clothing that will be made out of its skin. The skin must be carefully treated and decorated so that it is worthy of the Great Spirit. All parts of the deer should be shared among the Micmac people and anything not used should be hung on a tree so that it will not be desecrated. Thanksgiving must then be given to the Great Spirit for the use of the deer."

By the end of the 1400s, giant boats carrying unusually garbed people began to visit the Gulf of St. Lawrence. At first, these people with pale skins and hairy bodies came ashore only to acquire drinking water and firewood. They sometimes offered gifts of brightly coloured cloth, or left metal goods that were stronger than the copper the Micmac obtained form the mainland. Soon, the Micmac began to exchange gifts with these strangers, who especially seemed to like the Micmac's beaverskin clothing. The coming of these European visitors would soon change the ancient pattern of Micmac life.

THREE

The dunes at Cavendish on the north shore
Lionel Stevenson

ÎLE ST. JEAN
A NEGLECTED LAND

T he first European to visit the Island and leave a record of his trip was Jacques Cartier. Cartier and his men, some of whom were criminals released from jail for this voyage, set sail from St. Malo, France, in two vessels on April 20, 1534. After a remarkably quick trip, they arrived in Newfoundland twenty days later. Farther on, they sighted a group of great auks. "Some of these birds," Cartier wrote, "are as large as geese, being black and white with a beak like a crow. They are always in the water, being unable to fly, since they have tiny wings about half the size of your hand.... These birds are marvelously fat...and in less than half an hour our longboats were loaded with them. Each of our ships salted four or five casks, not to mention those we ate fresh." Easy to catch, tasty to eat, and good for fishing bait, the last great auk was killed in 1844.

After exploring the west coast of Newfoundland, Cartier sailed to the Magdalen Islands, where he encountered "many great beasts, like large oxen, which have two tusks in their jaws like elephants' tusks, and swim about in the water." Leaving these sea lions, Cartier sighted Prince Edward Island on June 29. He spent the next two days exploring the north coast, which he believed was part of the mainland. At Malpeque, Cartier wrote, "We went ashore in our longboats at several places, and among others at a fine river of little depth, where we caught sight of some Indians in their canoes who were crossing the river. On that account we named this river Canoe River." Cartier left a vivid description of the landscape. "We landed that day," he continued, "in four places to see the trees which were wonderfully beautiful and very fragrant. We discovered that there were cedars, yew-trees, pines, white elms, ash trees, willows and others, many of them unknown to us and all trees without fruit. The soil where there are no trees is also very rich and is covered with pease, white and red gooseberry bushes, strawberries, raspberries and wild oats like rye.... It is the best tempered region one can possibly see and the heat is considerable. There are many turtle-doves, wood-pigeons and other birds." This is the oldest existing description of the Island. It was initially published in Italian in 1556, in English in 1580, but not in French until 1598.

Cartier then turned northward into the Miramichi River and sailed to the Gaspé Peninsula. Here he erected a large cross, claimed the land for King Francis I of France, and returned to France with two young Iroquois captives. Except for European fishing boats that may have stopped to trade with the Micmac, or to collect firewood and drinking water, Europeans did not revisit P.E.I. for another sixty years.

Although the explorers did not find silks, spices, gold or silver in North America, the New World soon became very important to Europe. Fishermen from England, France, Spain, Portugal and Holland continued to come each spring to catch cod off the Grand Banks of Newfoundland, and in the Gulf of St. Lawrence and the Bay of Fundy. The cod were so plentiful that they sometimes slowed the fishermen's ships.

Fish was a major part of the diet of most Europeans. Roman Catholics were forbidden to eat meat on Fridays in memory of Christ's death on Good Friday. In addition, there were about one hundred and fifty days each year when Roman Catholics fasted without meat. Since fish was not considered meat, it was in great demand. Fish was also important to the economy of Great Britain, and the British government declared certain days fish days in order to encourage its consumption.

Before the cod were taken back to Europe, they had to be preserved. Salting was the easiest method of preserving fish, but salt was expensive. To reduce the amount of salt needed, British fishermen built wooden drying racks on the shore and put the fish out to dry in the summer sun. This practice of preserving fish was called the dry fishery. And so it was that Europeans came to inhabit the coastal areas on a seasonal basis.

While the fishermen were on shore, they took the opportunity to trade with the Micmac. The natives exchanged beaver, caribou, otter and other animal skins for guns, metal tools, axes, kettles and bright clothing. In Europe, beaver hats were in fashion, and everyone wanted one. And since styles kept changing, beaver skins were in constant demand. Instead of coming to North America in search of a route to Asia, Europeans now came for fish and furs. Soon the fishermen and the fur traders would be joined by settlers.

THE SETTLEMENT OF ACADIA

To help control both the fur trade and the fishing banks, France decided to establish a colony in North America. At the beginning of the 17th century, the King of France granted Sieur de Monts all of present-day Nova Scotia, New Brunswick, Prince Edward Island, and parts of Quebec and eastern United States. His grant also included the right to fish and trade with the Indians. In return, de Monts promised to bring settlers to the area.

The first group of French colonists, led by Champlain, Poutrincourt and de Monts, sailed into the Bay of Fundy in 1604. They decided to build a colony on a small island in the mouth of the St. Croix River. They had made a bad choice. The island had no fresh water and very little wood. To make matters worse, the winter weather that year was very severe. For most of the winter the island was blanketed by over a metre of snow. Icy winds whipped across the river and swept around the settlers' log cabins. Part way through the winter, the firewood ran out. Almost half of the eighty men died of scurvy and the cold.

In the spring, the remaining settlers moved across the Bay of Fundy to the mainland. Here they built the new colony of Port Royal. With the help of the Micmac, who provided the settlers with food and a cure for scurvy, Port Royal grew and prospered. Additional settlements were built along the shores and around the head of the Bay of Fundy. By the beginning of the 18th century, the population,

P. John Burden

which came mostly from the western part of France, numbered about eighteen hundred people and the inhabitants had developed a distinctive identity. The French settlers called their new home L'Acadie or Acadia, and before long the people living in present-day Nova Scotia, New Brunswick and Prince Edward Island were called Acadians. These people built dykes to drain the swamps and marshlands, and planted crops in the fertile soil.

Life was not always peaceful for the Acadians. For most of the 1600s, England and France were at war in Europe, and these conflicts frequently spread to North America. France argued that because Jacques Cartier was the first man to land in Acadia, it was French territory. England claimed that John Cabot was the first European to discover Acadia and that the land therefore belonged to it. The English called this area "Nova Scotia", which means "New Scotland" in Latin.

Although Acadia possessed good agricultural land, the region was more important for its position near the Grand Banks, and its strategic location between New France and New England. This is why Great Britain and France were willing to spill blood for Acadia. A British prime minister once declared that he would rather lose his right arm than surrender these fisheries, and a French minister announced that he would prefer to be stoned in the streets than lose them. To the south, Great Britain had established the Thirteen Colonies (part of the present-day United States). These British settlers feared the French and demanded that the mother country remove them by force. France wanted Acadia because it was located near the entrance of the St. Lawrence River and thus provided protection for the French colony of New France (Quebec). Finally, the valuable cod fisheries off the Grand Banks of Newfoundland could be controlled from Acadia. Acadia thus became a battleground between France and Great Britain in the 17th and 18th centuries. In its first one hundred years of existence, Acadia changed hands nine times and was attacked by British troops ten additional times. The Acadians were caught in the middle. They did not want to fight for either the French or the British. They wished to be left alone to tend their fields.

THE STRUGGLE FOR ACADIA

1605 —	*Port Royal established*
1613 —	*Port Royal burned to the ground*
1628 —	*Britain captures Port Royal*
1632 —	*Port Royal returned to France*
1654 —	*Britain captures Port Royal*
1670 —	*Given back to France*
1690 —	*Captured by Britain*
1697 —	*Returned to France*
1704 —	*British attack unsuccessful*
1707 —	*British attack unsuccessful*
1710 -—	*Port Royal captured by Britain, renamed Annapolis Royal*
1713 —	*Nova Scotia becomes a permanent British Colony*

A NEW BEGINNING

The year 1713 was a turning point in the history of Acadia. The war with Great Britain had gone poorly for France. In the Treaty of Utrecht which followed the defeat of France, Great Britain kept present-day Nova Scotia, New Brunswick and Newfoundland. The Acadians were told to either leave the colony or swear allegiance to the British crown. France retained New France, Île Royale (Cape Breton), Île St. Jean (Prince Edward Island), and the right to land its ships on the north coast of Newfoundland.

To protect New France and the Grand Banks, France decided to build a stone fortress on Île Royale. Construction began in 1720 and continued for twenty-five years. According to rumour, King Louis XV once joked that with all the money he had spent, he expected to see the fortress on the horizon. Louisbourg, as the fortress was named, was built on an ice-free harbour to control entry to the St. Lawrence River, to monitor the fishery and to protect Île St. Jean. Unfortunately, the land surrounding Louisbourg was infertile and the area was wind-swept and fog-bound for much of the year.

When Great Britain gained control of Acadia in 1713, France tried to persuade the Acadians to move to Île Royale. The more people living there, the stronger it would be against a British attack. Most Acadians, however, decided to remain in Nova Scotia. They had put too much work into their land to leave. Acadia was their homeland. Britain had captured Acadia several times before and had returned it to France, and the Acadians hoped that this would happen once again. The Acadians' love for their land was stronger than either their fear of the British or their obedience to France.

By 1719 it was obvious that few Acadians could be persuaded to leave for the poor agricultural land of Île Royale. King Louis XV therefore decided to open Île St. Jean for settlement. If the Acadians would not leave their farms for Île Royale, perhaps they would come to the Island, where the soil was more fertile. Île St. Jean might also provide food for the troops at Louisbourg. A new era was about to dawn for Prince Edward Island.

ÎLE ST. JEAN

Following Cartier's voyage in 1534, Europeans ignored Île St. Jean for almost two centuries. A few fishermen landed to obtain fresh water and dry their fish, but no one settled on the Island. In 1653, King Louis XIV of France granted control of the Island to Nicolas Denys in return for Denys' promise to settle eighty Roman Catholic families there. Ten years later, Denys had not brought any colonists to the Island and the King awarded it to Sieur Francois Doublet. When Doublet also failed to live up to his promises, King Louis XV bestowed Île St. Jean to Gabriel Gauthier, and later to Comte (Count) de Saint Pierre in 1719.

In April 1720, approximately two hundred and fifty colonists set out from France with supplies of grain, livestock, tools and clothing. Four months later the ships sailed into Port LaJoye (across the Hillsborough Harbour from present-day Charlottetown). In the next few years, the colonists established several settlements along the coast. The largest settlements were at St. Peter's Harbour, Tracadie, Savage Harbour, Malpeque and Trois Rivières (present-day Brudenell Point). Port LaJoye became the capital of the Island. A garrison of thirty ill-equipped men remained at the fort to guard the entrance to the harbour. Unfortunately for Île St. Jean, the King of France was not particularly interested in the Island. It was Louisbourg that was important to France. As a result, Île St. Jean played second fiddle to Louisbourg. The Island was thus colonized to grow food for the soldiers on Île Royale. The mainland Acadians, however, did not find the Island as fertile as their own land, and by 1630 the number of settlers had only grown to 325 people.

JEAN PIERRE ROMA

Jean Pierre Roma was one of the few people at this time who thought that Île St. Jean had a bright future. He was born in France in the 17th century, but no one knows exactly where or when. Where and when he died is also unknown. We do know that Roma founded a colony at Trois Rivières and became one of the most important men on Île St. Jean.

Roma was a fascinating character. He was honest and hardworking. He was also stubborn, quick to anger and hated criticism. Roma was full of dreams for the Island's future, but his plans for Trois Rivières were destroyed by bad luck and poor interpersonal communications. In 1731, King Louis XV gave the land drained by the Cardigan, Brudenell and Montague Rivers to a French company called the Company of the East. In return for this land, the company agreed to establish a colony on the Island. Roma, who was one of the Company's directors, arrived on the Island in 1732 with about three hundred people. He chose the land at Trois Rivières to establish his colony.

In the following two years, Roma personally looked after the settlement's growth. To improve the harbour, the men levelled the shoreline and built a pier, which meant moving more than 195 metric tonnes of stone by hand. The men cleared the nearby fields of timber, removed over six thousand stumps, levelled the land, and built nine houses, two of which were twenty-four metres long. The settlers planted vegetable gardens around every building, and surrounded the gardens with brush-wood fences to keep animals out. Cabbages, turnips, wheat and peas were staple crops, and fishermen harvested the sea.

The colonists traded their goods with the other settlements on the Island. The route by sea, however, was long, and the frequent storms were especially dangerous for the small fishing vessels. If the colony were to survive, roads had to be built. Roma thus set his men to work cutting two-metre-wide bush paths through the wilderness to join Trois Rivières with Cardigan, Souris, Sturgeon River, St. Peter's Harbour, and the capital at Port LaJoye. Writing about the path from Trois Rivières to Port LaJoye, Roma said, "Most of the trees lying on the ground across the road have been left where they lie, since it is easy enough to step over them."

Despite Roma's two years of hard work, the other directors of the Company of the East were not pleased with the colony's progress. They wanted profits, but in the first year Trois Rivières had cost twice as much money to operate as it had earned.

Unwilling to weather a few lean years, the directors refused to pay for more provisions, and blamed Roma for the colony's lack of success. They claimed, for example, that Roma used fishermen to

THE TRACADIE FAMILIES OF 1752

In one small area, Tracadie Harbour, eight families had settled on the west side of the harbour, and had cleared the land to the east of the harbour for their crops of wheat, barley and peas. Their livestock grazed on the grassy meadows to the south.

The families made their living by farming the land and fishing for cod. Often, three generations lived together in one household, and all family members assisted in the numerous tasks of these labour-intensive activities.

The census of 1752 was carried out on the Island by the Sieur de la Roque. He was asked to record the names, ages and professions of all settlers and their children, and the amount of cleared land and number of livestock. Further instructions asked him to inspect the coast for places where troops could be most easily landed; to give the size and condition of harbours; and to conduct "a general survey of everything."

FAMILY NAME	NUMBER OF CHILDREN
Galland (Jacques)	7
Boudrot (Charles)	4
Bourg (Charles)	12
Boudrot (Pierre)	2
Bourg (Michel)	7
Boudrot (Francois)	6
Boudrot (Claude)	6
Belliveaux (Louis)	6

build roads rather than allowing them to fish. He spent too much money on the colony, when he should have been looking for ways of making a profit. Roma argued with the settlers and destroyed their enthusiasm—or so the directors stated. Roma's attitude toward the people was perhaps best seen by his refusal to attend weddings and baptisms. These events were the centre of the colony's social life, and his reluctance to attend such celebrations upset many of the settlers. When the Company decided to rid itself of this "burden", Roma bought the Company's land on Île St. Jean in 1737.

ROMA, THE PRIESTS, AND BAD LUCK

The Company had sent two priests to Trois Rivières with the first settlers. Roma disliked them both. He especially distrusted Abbé de Bierne, who was just as stubborn as Roma. De Bierne insisted that the people should not be forced to work on Sundays and other holy days. Roma stated that there was too much work to be done to allow for rest on Sundays, and argued that he had the King's authority to make laws for his colony. De Bierne claimed to have divine authority and informed the settlers that they were to follow his instructions in matters of religion. After a bitter struggle, Roma forced the Abbé to leave. Shortly afterwards, Roma dismissed the remaining priest.

Bad luck also plagued the settlement. In 1736, fire destroyed most of the crops. Two years later, a plague of field mice ate the entire crop. Not long after this, Roma's cargo vessel was shipwrecked. These disasters forced Roma to borrow money to keep the colony afloat. Finally, just when the future began to look promising, British troops attacked Trois Rivières in 1745. Having only one cannon for defence, Roma and his settlers fled into the woods, and they watched helplessly from the forest as the British set their homes on fire and loaded the colony's livestock, tools and grain aboard ship, and set sail.

Roma's dreams were shattered. Faced with starvation, Roma sailed to Quebec. He remained there for three years before going to the West Indies. Jean Pierre Roma wanted to return to Île St. Jean to start again. However, he had no money and the French officials would not help him. Roma never returned. His work would be continued by others.

WAR AGAIN

The British attack at Trois Rivières in 1745 was part of a general war between France and Great Britain. As had happened so often before, the fighting began in Europe and spread around the world. Great Britain wanted to gain complete control over both the Atlantic fisheries and the fur trade along the St. Lawrence River. The British colonists living in New England wished to stop the French settlers and their Micmac allies from raiding and looting their villages. To achieve both goals, Louisbourg, France's fortress on Île Royale, had to be captured.

In 1745, with the help of the American colonies, Great Britain used its superior naval power to capture Louisbourg. Some of its ships then sailed from New England to Île St. Jean and destroyed the French settlements at Trois Rivières and Port LaJoye. Roma's colony, as we have seen, did not resist. At Port LaJoye, the small garrison was undermanned and poorly equipped, and the soldiers retreated into the interior. As the British soldiers advanced into the woods, they were ambushed by a band of Micmac who had joined the French troops. The British invaders were driven back to their boats, and later returned to Louisbourg. They left behind burned houses and crops—the ruins of the Island's capital. In exchange for six prisoners captured by the Island Acadians, Great Britain agreed to allow the Acadians to remain on Île St. Jean for one more year.

THE PEACE TREATY

The war lasted four years. Neither side was completely victorious. Great Britain captured Île Royale in North America, but lost territory in other parts of the world. At the peace talks in 1748, the British traded Louisbourg for the Indian state of Madras. In North America, the situation reverted to where it had been in 1713.

Now, for the first time, France began to take a serious interest in Île St. Jean, and plans to encourage the Acadians on the mainland, which was still a British possession, to move to this French island. At first, not many came. However, when Great Britain demanded that the Acadians promise to fight in all future North American wars against France, many Acadians decided to move to Île St. Jean. New settlements began at present-day Pownal, Orwell, Pinette, Crapaud, Tryon, Covehead and Malpeque. Although Île St. Jean was still second in importance to Louisbourg, the Island was finally showing signs of real progress.

Between 1748 and 1751 the population tripled to over two thousand people. To ensure that the garrison at Louisbourg was well-fed, King Louis XV ordered the Islanders to refrain from fishing because, he declared, it detracted from farming. The Island, however, had few meadows and the Acadians were forced to clear the forest, which was a back-breaking job compared to erecting dykes and draining marshland. The typical farm had pigs, sheep, oxen, rams, hens, lambs and cows—but only a few of each. Wheat, peas and oats were the most common crops (potatoes were not yet grown on the Island). Île St. Jean, however, never fulfilled its role as a breadbasket for Louisbourg. Forest fires, wheat rust, and plagues of mice and grasshoppers meant that Louisbourg often had to supply the settlers with food, lest they starve. The Acadians' dietary staples consisted of pea soup, wheaten bread or porridge, rations of salted beef, pork, mutton and fowl, maple syrup, herbs and garden vegetables, fish and game. The men smoked tobacco, and the women chewed spruce gum, which aided digestion and cleansed the teeth.

THE MICE INVASION

The Acadian settlers on P.E.I. often had plagues of grasshoppers, mosquitoes and mice. The mice were a constant problem. They were black with short legs and flat paws. They lived in the forests and stored seeds, nuts and grasses for the winter. Every six weeks the female produced a litter of between ten and twelve young. When the snow was deep for several winters in a row, the mice population multiplied rapidly. In spring, the starving mice marched out of the forest in long narrow columns.

They ate everything in their way. The mice destroyed crops and ate the food set aside for livestock. They swarmed over the grassy fields. When the mice came to a river, those in the front were pushed on by those behind, and the river became choked with dead bodies. So numerous were these tiny invaders that nearby ships were slowed by the huge masses of drowned mice.

Plagues of mice destroyed crops in 1724, 1728, 1738, and 1749. Each time this happened the settlers had to rely on Louisbourg for food and seeds. The town of Souris, which means "mouse" in French, was named in memory of these plagues.

FOUR

THE MICMAC AND THE ACADIANS

The first Europeans to contact the Micmac were fishermen who had come to catch cod. In the 17th century, France established trading posts in present-day Nova Scotia and New Brunswick. Because there were no trading posts on Île St. Jean at this time, the Island Micmac canoed to the mainland posts. They also traded with French ships that anchored offshore in the summer. Firing their guns into the air, the French traders greeted the Micmac with great ceremony.

The Europeans believed that they were superior to the Micmac. The natives wore few clothes and their technology seemed inferior to European guns and sophisticated tools. Unable to understand the Micmac language, Europeans judged the natives by their material possessions, and found them wanting. French priests, unfamiliar with Micmac beliefs, decided that they were heathens who had to be converted and civilized. Not surprisingly, the Micmac considered themselves superior to the white men. European men were unable to canoe or snowshoe very far before becoming exhausted. They performed such menial tasks as carrying water and collecting firewood. And their bodies and faces were covered with "ugly" masses of hair. Although the Micmac and the French each believed that they were the superior people, they usually lived together in peace because each had something the other wanted.

The Micmac were generous and willingly shared their belongings with the strangers. The first Acadian settlers had no idea what was safe to eat. They did not know where to settle, how to travel over the deep snow, or where to cross the swiftly flowing rivers. The Micmac acted as guides. They taught the Acadians how to use canoes, toboggans, snowshoes and moccasins. They showed the settlers how to hunt and where to fish. When the settlers ran out of food, the Micmac fed them. When they became sick, the Micmac showed them which roots and herbs would cure them. Many of the first explorers and settlers suffered and even died from scurvy. The natives taught them how to make a broth from the needles and bark of the white cedar tree to prevent scurvy.

Because there were so few Europeans in Acadia, the Micmac continued to hunt and fish as they wished. When Great Britain won control of Nova Scotia, France tried to convince the Micmac to relocate to Cape Breton or even P.E.I., but they refused. Lack of power, rather than lack of desire, prevented the French from actively attempting to control the Micmac. The priests had the most influence over the Micmac. In order to civilize and convert the natives, the priests attempted to convince them to stop their nomadic ways and adopt agricultural pursuits. In the early 1730s, Abbés Gaulin and Courtin established a settlement at Malpeque for the Île St. Jean Micmac. The natives, however, were not interested in forsaking their old way of life, and since the priest visited them only once a year, the mission was never very successful. The French had the most extensive contact with the Micmac during the festivities of Saint Anne's Day (Saint Anne was the Micmac patron saint), and the annual summer visit of the governor of Île Royale to Port LaJoye to distribute presents. The French authorities took advantage of these meetings to gather information about the activities of the English, to gain the Micmac's goodwill, and to incite them against the British.

A Micmac chief related the following story to a Roman Catholic missionary not long after Champlain left Acadia.

Why do men who are 5 or 6 feet high need houses 60 or 80 feet high? Have you as much cleverness and ingenuity as we who carry our houses with us, so that we may lodge wherever we please? We are at home everywhere, because we set up our wigwams wherever we go, without asking permission of anyone. But we are much happier than you, for we are content with the little that we have. If France, as you say, is an earthly paradise, why did you leave it?... Now tell me this one little thing, if you have any sense: which of the two is wiser and happier—he who labours without ceasing that only obtains with great trouble enough to live on, or he who rests in comfort that finds all that he needs in the pleasure of hunting and fishing.

The fur trade was probably the most important reason why these two peoples lived in peace. The Micmac exchanged beaver pelts, bear and moose hides for French guns, copper kettles and iron tools. These manufactured goods cost the European traders very little, whereas the furs were worth a lot of money in Europe. The French traders believed that they profited more from this trade. The Micmac also thought that they had made the better deal. In exchange for goods that they could not obtain elsewhere, the Micmac often traded the clothes off their backs. French hat-makers preferred these used pelts to freshly skinned furs because the grease from the Micmac's bodies made them more pliable.

The Micmac traded to make their lives easier. Iron knives and axes were stronger and remained sharp longer than stone or bone tools. Muskets were better than arrows because they could kill from a greater distance. Copper kettles were more durable than wood or stone cooking vessels. It was easier to trade for cloth than to make clothes from hides. Glass beads, brandy, tobacco, beans, flour, biscuits, iron harpoons, metal fish hooks and blankets were also desirable trade items. In addition to furs, the Micmac traded their handicrafts to the French. Micmac wood, bone, and stone carvings were valued in Europe for their designs and decorations. Birch bark was embroidered with moosehair or covered with porcupine-quill designs, and sold as souvenirs. Gradually the Micmac women began to use European techniques and materials in their artwork.

These trading partners soon became military allies; in fact, the word "Micmac" means "ally". The Micmac acted as scouts for the French soldiers, raided British settlements, and captured British ships in the harbour. The Micmac, however, always remained independent, and decided for themselves when to fight and when to hide or retreat. The Europeans considered the natives' refusal to stay and fight in a losing cause to be cowardly, whereas the Micmac believed the Europeans' obedience to authority, even in the face of certain death, to be the greatest of follies.

THE MICMAC LOSE CONTROL
OF THEIR LIFESTYLE

As the number of Acadian settlers grew, the Micmac began to face serious problems. Perhaps the worst problem was disease. Europeans brought with them such diseases as smallpox, influenza, chicken pox, whooping cough, tuberculosis, syphilis and scarlet fever. The Micmac had never been exposed to these diseases before and their bodies had not built up an immunity to them. Even measles could be deadly. Although no one questions that the Micmac population declined precipitously after contact with the Europeans, anthropologists differ about which factor had the greatest effect on their decreased numbers. Some researchers, for example, argue that the Micmac's growing dependence on alcohol and French foods weakened their resistance to certain diseases. Whatever the cause, the Micmac died by the thousands. No one knows exactly how many died, but one estimate places the number at ten Micmac dead for every one who survived.

The Micmac shamans, who were the communities' doctors as well as their spiritual leaders, could not cure these new diseases. As a result, the natives began to doubt the power of their shamans. This made it easier for the French missionaries to convert the Micmac to Christianity. When animals became items of trade rather than life-giving food, the spiritual bond that had once united the hunter and his prey disintegrated, and the natives began to adopt a more materialistic attitude towards their environment. Energy spent hunting and trapping was time away from traditional pursuits. The Micmac soon became torn between loyalty to their own spiritual beliefs and the religious ideas of the Catholic priests. Their culture was being slowly undermined.

The introduction of alcohol as a trade item was another problem that the Europeans brought to the Micmac. Despite the complaints of the Catholic priests, the Europeans traded brandy with the natives. The Micmac were not accustomed to alcohol, which had a detrimental effect on them. Some researchers suggest that the natives' lack of resistance to alcohol was due to a slightly different body chemistry than the Europeans. Other academics explain the Micmac's tendency to become drunk on their religious beliefs, which emphasized achieving a trance-like state before communing with the spirits.

By 1758, the Micmac had become reliant upon the fur traders for most of their food, clothes and tools. To obtain these goods, the Micmac had to bring in animal hides and pelts. As the demand for furs increased, more animals were killed and the amount of game steadily declined. Thus, when the European traders deserted their fur trading posts in the Maritime region for the more profitable beaver lands in western Canada, the Micmac were no longer able to feed and clothe themselves as they had done in the past.

The "good old days" had disappeared. The arrival of the Europeans had changed the Micmac's way of life. Soon there were more Acadian settlers than Micmac, and the Micmac became dependent upon them for survival.

FIVE

The Expulsion of the Acadians
Parks Canada

THE END OF THE FRENCH PERIOD

By the middle of the 18th century, Great Britain was becoming more and more worried about the Acadians in Nova Scotia. The British distrusted them. The Acadians were Roman Catholics, spoke French, and listened to their French-born priests. Five times since 1713 the British governors of Acadia had attempted to persuade the Acadians to swear an oath of allegiance to the British monarch. Each time the Acadians refused.

In 1755, the British governor of Nova Scotia, Charles Lawrence, decided to solve this problem. He ordered the Acadians to sign an oath of loyalty to Great Britain or be deported from the colony. The Acadians didn't want to fight for either country. They considered themselves neither French nor British, but Acadians. In the past they had remained neutral, and they promised to do so in all future wars. Lawrence, however, did not believe the Acadians, and ordered their deportation. Thousands of settlers were rounded up, herded onto ships, and sent to other British colonies. To escape this fate, some two thousand Acadians fled to Île St. Jean.

This exodus brought total confusion to Île St. Jean. In less than three years the population almost tripled. The previous five years had yielded only one good crop on the Island, so there was not enough food for everyone. Many of the newcomers had arrived with only the clothes they were wearing. Families wandered from barn to barn seeking food and shelter. Life was miserable, but the Acadians believed that even this life was preferable to deportation to a strange land.

The next year, Great Britain and France were again at war. Once more, the fighting in Europe spilled over into North America. Many of the young men on Île St. Jean went to Louisbourg to help defend the fortress. In July 1758, however, Louisbourg surrendered to the British fleet. Lord Rollo, one of the British commanders, then sailed to Île St. Jean with four warships. His orders were to remove all the Acadians, build a fort on the Island, destroy the crops and kill the livestock. The purpose of the last two orders was to discourage the Acadians from returning.

Lord Rollo sailed into Hillsborough Bay on August 17, 1758. The Acadians had only a few cannons and muskets. They had no chance of victory. When the inhabitants of Port LaJoye saw Lord Rollo's ships approaching, the women and children hid in the forest and buried their personal belongings and religious ornaments. The more daring inhabitants made their way to the north shore, and with the

EVANGELINE

In 1847, Henry Longfellow wrote his famous poem, *Evangeline*. In this poem, Evangeline Bellefontaine, a maiden of seventeen, is separated from her lover, Gabriel Lajeunesse, during the deportation from Grand Pré, and the two lovers spend the rest of their lives searching for each other. After years of sorrow, she finds him again. But he is a broken old man, and dies in her arms.

Half-way down to the shore
Evangeline waited in silence,
Not overcome with grief, but strong in the hour of affliction,
Calmly and sadly she waited, until the procession approached her,
And she held the face of Gabriel pale with emotion.
Tears then filled her eyes, and, eagerly running to meet him,
Clasped she his hands, and laid her head on his shoulder, and whispered,
"Gabriel! be of good cheer! for if we love one another,
Nothing in truth, can harm us, whatever mischances may happen!"
.... Thus to the Gaspereau's mouth moved on that mournful procession.
There disorder prevailed, and the tumult and stir of embarking.
Busily plied the freighted boats; and in the confusion
Wives were torn from their husbands, and mothers, too late, saw their children
Left on the land, extending their arms, with wildest entreaties.
So unto separate ships were Basil and Gabriel carried,
While in despair on the shore Evangeline stood with her father.

help of the Micmac, escaped to New France or to the French islands of St. Pierre and Miquelon off the Newfoundland coast. The garrison at Port LaJoye surrendered without firing a shot.

The British soldiers eventually caught most of the Acadians and herded them to Port LaJoye. These prisoners, who had not fought in the war, begged to remain on the Island, but the British ignored their pleas and shipped about three thousand dispirited Acadians to Louisbourg. They were allowed to pack only their clothes, bedding, and a few personal belongings. Dogs, horses, tools, dishes and the rest of their possessions were left behind for the conquerors. From Louisbourg, the Acadians were crowded aboard ships and sent to France. Approximately seven hundred Acadians who embarked on the *Duke William* and the *Violet* perished at sea in December 1758. A violent Atlantic storm damaged both ships. Before the men on board the *Duke William* could aid their sister vessel, another squall sep-

THE ORIGINAL ACADIANS IN 1763

Approximately nine out of every ten Acadian people on Prince Edward Island today are descended from the families listed in this chart. These families were among those who had avoided capture by the British in 1758.

ACADIAN FAMILY NAMES ACCORDING TO THE 1798 CENSUS

Arsenault	Chiasson	Doiron
Doucet	Gauthier	Bourque
Gaudet	Martin	Blaquiere
Buote	Richard	Michel
Poirier	Cheverie	Muise
Pineau	Des Roches	St-Jean
Pitre	Blanchard	Roussel
Landry	Gallant	Downing
Longueepee	Le Clerc	Gautreau
Aucoin	Bernard	Le Brun

Some Acadians later Anglicized their names: Aucoin became Wedge, Poirier became Perry, Pitre became Peters, LeClerc became Le Clair, and Bourque became Burke.

arated the two ships and all four hundred passengers were drowned. A similar fate awaited the *Duke William*, which began taking on more water than the men, including the Acadians, could pump out. The captain distributed the remaining liquor to the people, and kept the ship afloat by filling casks with air and placing them below deck. Twice, vessels approached the stricken ship only to sail away. "Driven from the greatest joy to the utmost despair, death now appeared more dreadful." When all seemed lost, the Acadians apparently requested their captors to take the lifeboats and leave them aboard, there not being enough boats for everyone. Reluctantly, the captain agreed. Just before the *Duke William* sank, four Acadians discovered a small boat and escaped. "The *Duke William* (according to their report) swam till it felt calm, and as she went down her decks blew up. The noise was like the explosion of a gun, or a loud clap of thunder."

We can only imagine the feelings of those Acadians who arrived safely in France. Most of them had never been to France. For years they had struggled in Acadia to clear the forests, plant crops and build homes. Now all their hard work was in the hands of the hated British. The Acadians would have to begin a new life in a different land. During the next twenty-five years, some Acadians returned to Acadia, others remained in the West Indies, the United States (some becoming the Cajuns of Louisiana), and as far away as the Falkland Islands.

Some Acadians on Île St. Jean managed to stay hidden from Lord Rollo's troops. Approximately thirty families near Malpeque escaped deportation. Most of the present Acadian population of Prince Edward Island is descended from these families, or from the deported Acadians who later returned to the Island.

On October 7, 1763, the war between Great Britain and France officially ended. North America became a British possession. Île St. Jean was renamed St. John's Island. At Fort Amherst, which was built on the site of Port LaJoye, the British flag was raised on Island soil. France's control of the Island had ended.

SIX

George
the
Third,
King of
Great
Britain
PAC

SETTLING THE ISLAND

THE LOTTERY AND THE LANDLORDS

Great Britain now owned St. John's Island, but did not know what to do with it. There was good fishing in the area; but how valuable were its other resources? Although no one knew the answers to these questions, many people in Great Britain were willing to gamble that the Island was valuable. Almost as soon as the ink was dry on the treaty, King George III was flooded with requests for land. Lord Egmont, for example, asked the King to give him St. John's Island as his own personal island.

George III decided to learn more about his new colonies in North America before making any decisions, and hired Samuel Jan Holland in 1764 to survey St. John's Island, Cape Breton and the Magdalens. Captain Holland was well-suited to the task. He was a military engineer and a skilled cartographer. Holland had fought with the British soldiers when they captured Louisbourg and hoped that Great Britain would now settle the conquered lands. The following account is based on Captain Holland's description of his work on St. John's Island.

SAMUEL HOLLAND ON ST. JOHN'S ISLAND

We arrived at Hillsborough Bay in the fall of 1764. Fortunately, I had been warned to bring extra food and building materials, because there was no place for us to stay. Fort Amherst, which was built by Lord Rollo, is falling down. My men immediately built a house near the seashore [Rocky Point] from the ruins of some old houses. It is a good spot to chart the stars, but it is not very comfortable.

I wished to start surveying as soon as possible, but the naval commander refused use of some of his equipment, and then Marie Josephte bore me a handsome son. I wouldn't be surprised if John Frederick wasn't the first British baby born on St. John's Island. When we were finally able to work, it was winter. The weather was so cold that one soldier froze to death and several others suffered from frost-bitten hands and feet.

I divided the men into small groups of five people. Each field group loaded their toboggans with warm coats, blankets, and food and drink for eight days. I hired some Acadians to guide us, and we used their dogs to pull the toboggans. I feel sorry for the Acadians. They are treated like enemy prisoners by the soldiers, and they are very poor.

Every day I made notes about the wildlife, forests, climate, rivers, harbours and the fertility of the soil. The results were put on a huge map that is taller than I am.

The most difficult problem was deciding which location would make the best capital. The choice was between the villages I have named Charlottetown, Georgetown and Princetown. All have excellent harbours—which is very important for transportation and defence. Princetown has the best location for fishing. Georgetown's three rivers provide excellent routes inland.

I finally chose Charlottetown. It is near the middle of the Island and its three rivers provide easy travel into the interior. A small stream runs through Charlottetown and provides pure drinking water. The site is also easily defended. The cannons at Fort Amherst control the harbour. If enemy troops do land, they must cross one of the two rivers before attacking the capital. In addition, Charlottetown is closest to the mainland and is thus best suited for trading with Nova Scotia and Quebec.

**Captain S.J. Holland,
1765**

Samuel Holland finished his survey and moved on to the Magdalens. Although the map contained a few mistakes, the survey formed the basis of the present division of land. He divided the Island into 67 townships or lots of about eight thousand hectares (twenty thousand acres) each, three counties (Kings, Queens and Prince), and fourteen parishes.

THE LOTTERY

The British government was still not certain what to do with St. John's Island. It was deluged with requests for large parcels of the Island from many wealthy and important people. Every applicant was interviewed and told to write a letter explaining why he deserved the land. The government then selected about one hundred people to take part in a lottery. On July 23, 1767, nearly the entire Island was given away. The land was chosen by lot. Each person's name was written on a slip of paper and placed in a box. The first name picked (Philip Stevens) received township number one, the second name chosen was given township number two. This continued until all 67 townships had been granted. The King kept township 66, and reserved additional land for schools, churches and for county capitals Georgetown, Charlottetown and Princetown. Lots 40 and 59 were granted prior to the lottery.

THE LANDLORDS

The British government required the new owners to settle the land, to pay for the construction of roads and jails, and to provide salaries for the judges, sheriffs, and government leaders. Each new landlord had to pay a small annual fee, called a quit rent, for his land. The more valuable the land, the higher the quit rent. Within ten years the owners were also obligated to settle one Protestant person (but not from Great Britain) for every 44.5 hectares they were given. Roman Catholics were not wanted as settlers because Britain distrusted them—especially after the recent wars with Catholic France. If these terms were not fulfilled, the government reserved the right to repossess the land.

Very few owners, however, either paid their quit rents to the government or brought over settlers. Many landlords were not interested in settling St. John's Island. They had asked for the land solely to make money. Within the first ten years, one-quarter of the lots were re-sold, but few settlers were brought to the Island.

SETTLING THE ISLAND

Although most of the new landlords lost interest in the Island, several owners did attempt to colonize their lands. Sir James Montgomery founded settlements at Covehead and Stanhope. Robert Stewart sent Scottish settlers to Malpeque. Captain John MacDonald established a colony at Tracadie. Robert Clark brought colonists to New London. Samuel Holland sponsored a few families at Cape Traverse, and Thomas Des Brisay sent nine families to Lots 31 and 33. From 1770 to 1775, almost one thousand people came to

Prince Edward Island. Although the landlords' leases required that only Protestants be settled on the Island, the majority of these immigrants were Scottish Roman Catholics. Other settlers were mostly English and Scottish Protestants.

The next large group of immigrants came in 1784. The American Revolution (1775-1783) had just ended and many people who were still loyal to Great Britain decided to leave the United States for British territory. Roughly six hundred of these "Loyalists" came to settle in Bedeque, Orwell, Tryon, Vernon River and East Point. Several hundred Loyalists left the Island when they discovered that they could not buy land. Most landlords would rent to the Loyalists, but would not sell them land. Those Loyalists who did remain contributed their skills to the colony's development.

SIR JAMES MONTGOMERY'S SETTLEMENTS, 1769-1788

James Montgomery was one of the most important politicians and businessmen in Scotland. In 1769 he became interested in establishing a flax farm on P.E.I. and soon gained control of almost 40,470 hectares of land. He hired David Lawson, a Scottish flax farmer, to manage this farm. The farm work was to be performed by fifty servants, who agreed to serve for four years, after which time Montgomery promised to rent them land at inexpensive rates.

The Scottish settlers arrived at Stanhope Cove in June 1770. They faced incredible problems. Stanhope was a complete wilderness. There were no people or buildings, and the only nourishment available was oatmeal, berries and seafood. A shipload of food finally arrived, but the horses and farm equipment never did come. Because there were no farm implements available on the Island, the settlers had to make all their own tools.

Slowly the colonists cleared the land, planted seeds, and built a water mill to grind grain. Two years later, the mill was destroyed by fire. Lawson rebuilt the mill, but the very day it was completed, the mill burned down again. On the third attempt, the land around the mill was cleared to protect it from fire. A short time later, the mill dam was destroyed by a flood. Lawson also had problems with his workers. In the first year, one man was crushed when a large pine tree he was chopping fell on him. Two other men drowned. Finally, just when the flax farm began to make money, the servants' contracts expired, and they scattered across the Island.

Sir James Montgomery became worried about the lack of profits, and wrote Lawson for an explanation. However, the American Revolution had begun and Montgomery was unable to correspond with Lawson for six years. The war also stopped all immigration to the Island. Sir James finally contacted his farm manager, and dismissed him. James Montgomery had lost faith in the Island and now turned his attention elsewhere.

JOHN MACDONALD AND THE GLENALADALE SETTLERS

Captain MacDonald's reasons for settling the Tracadie area (Lot 36) in 1772 were quite different from Montgomery's motives for colonizing Stanhope. The Roman Catholic Church in Scotland asked MacDonald to transport Catholic tenant farmers to North America. The Catholic religion had been illegal in Scotland for over one hundred and fifty years, but it had managed to survive in the isolated

Scottish Highlands. Several uprisings against the British King, however, convinced the British government to take more severe measures against the Highland Catholics. At this time, the owner of South Uist Island in the Hebrides decided to convert the Catholics on his property to Protestantism. A Protestant teacher was hired to convert the children, who were forced to eat meat during Lent and to copy anti-Catholic sentences in their writing books. When other islands in the Hebrides began to adopt these practices, the Catholic bishops became alarmed, and sought for a way to end this religious persecution.

The Scottish Protestant landowners in the Hebrides had a serious weakness. To prosper they needed a large number of tenants to farm their lands. The Catholic Church, therefore, decided to force the owners to grant better conditions by threatening to transport the tenants to North America, and turned to John MacDonald to organize such an expedition.

Captain John, as he was later called on Prince Edward Island, was well educated. He could speak seven languages. He was a proud and fearless man, whose hot temper and critical statements often created enemies. On one occasion, he was challenged to a duel. MacDonald was a devout Roman Catholic and a proud Highland Scot who wished to help his fellow Catholics and preserve Scottish culture and ideas in the New World.

John MacDonald sent his brother Donald to America to search for a suitable place to establish a colony. Favourable rumours about the success of Sir James Montgomery's flax farm, and exaggerated stories about the rich soil and mild climate, convinced the Catholic bishops to follow through with their plans to send some of their flock to the Island. MacDonald bought Lot 36 from Montgomery and began to recruit settlers. The Protestant owners in the Hebrides did not want their tenants to leave, and spread rumours that anyone who went to the Island would be sold into slavery. Partly as a result of these rumours, only 210 people agreed to leave for the Island in 1772. Captain John remained in Scotland to look after the finances and recruit more people. His brother, who had taken seventeen families to Scotchfort (Lot 36) the previous year, was put in charge of the settlement.

The threat to remove all the Catholic tenant farmers from the Hebrides had the desired result. To prevent more Highland settlers from leaving, Protestant landowners lowered their rents and promised to allow freedom of religion.

At Scotchfort, Prince Edward Island, however, the settlers were unhappy with the wilderness conditions. Some people talked about moving to Nova Scotia, where they could own their own farms. A Catholic priest wrote, "There is no money, no clothes, and no meat unless we pay four times what it is worth. It breaks my heart that my poor friends who were doing well before they left Scotland are now upon the brink of great misery and poverty."

The next year, Captain John arrived with more colonists and supplies of grain and food. The colony survived. As a landlord, Captain John encouraged his tenants to continue their traditional farming methods. Although this policy helped to preserve Highland culture on the Island, raising livestock was not the most profitable farming activity. MacDonald also kept the best land for his family and refused to rent or sell it to his tenants.

THE SELKIRK SETTLEMENT, 1803–1804

The American Revolution (1775–1783) isolated Prince Edward Island from Great Britain and stopped all further immigration. Despite the settlement schemes of Montgomery, MacDonald, and a few other landlords, by 1783 the total population of the Island was only about twelve hundred. Of the 67 lots, 48 were unpopulated. By 1805, however, the population had grown to about seven thousand. Thomas Douglas, Earl of Selkirk, brought the largest single group of settlers.

Thomas Douglas had not expected to inherit his father's fortune. His four older brothers were first in line. By 1799, however, all four had died, and Thomas Douglas became the Earl of Selkirk. He now had enough money to carry out his dreams. Despite poor health, Selkirk was a bundle of nervous energy. He could never sit still, and his mind was always busy planning projects. The three adjectives that probably best described his personality were impetuous, stubborn and ambitious. Selkirk would often commit himself to a project before he had carefully thought it out. Yet, once he decided on something, he kept at it until it was finished.

In 1802, to do something useful for the world, Selkirk decided to establish a colony in the New World. The decision to settle Highland Scots on Prince Edward Island was the result of a series of accidents, rather than a deliberate choice. Selkirk initially wanted to transport poor Irishmen to Louisiana. When this failed, he considered shipping Highlanders to the United States. The British government objected to this plan, so Selkirk decided upon Upper Canada (present-day Ontario). Only weeks before the Scottish families were to leave, the British government withdrew its offer of free land in Upper Canada. After a week of furious dealings, Selkirk bought 32,370 hectares on Prince Edward Island. Early in the summer of 1803, about eight hundred Highlanders set sail for the Orwell-Point Prim area aboard the *Polly*, the *Dykes* and the *Oughton*. This was the largest of all the settlement schemes on P.E.I.

The Scots were an obvious choice as potential settlers. Unemployment was high in Scotland, and the crops had failed several years in a row. Scottish tenant farmers were being forced off their lands and replaced by sheep ranching. Selkirk did most of his recruiting in the Hebrides, particularly on the Isle of Skye.

These settlers experienced the same sorts of problems that had plagued earlier immigrants. Lord Selkirk, aboard the *Dykes*, had planned to arrive first, but the *Polly* landed two days before him (the *Oughton*, eighteen days later). Despite these problems, the Selkirk settlers prospered. Their success encouraged others to come. One of the reasons for this success was that Selkirk felt responsible for his settlers and tried to help them get established. Instead of encouraging the colonists to spread out, he attempted to keep them together so as to preserve old values and customs and help one another.

Selkirk divided the land into long, narrow strips, extending to the shore. The distance between families was seldom more than 1.6 km. Selkirk also lifted the people's spirits by selling rather than renting the land. The settlers knew that if they worked hard, they would be able to buy their own land. Equally important, the Highlanders who came with Selkirk had been among the most prosperous tenant farmers in Scotland. They came to the Island because they wished to. Such people were more likely to do well than poor tenant farmers who had been forced to leave Scotland.

Selkirk remained only a few months on the Island. His future contacts with the Island were generally unhappy. His agent on the Island did not keep him informed about the colony's progress, and sold the valuable timber on his property without Selkirk's approval. Selkirk gradually lost interest in the Island and turned his attention to establishing the Red River colony near present-day Winnipeg.

SEVEN

Acadian Home in Rustico
Robert Harris

SHIPWRECKS, HARDSHIPS
AND PIONEER LIFE

It is hard for us to imagine the difficulties and problems faced by the first immigrants to Prince Edward Island. The voyage across the Atlantic often tested the endurance of the hardiest passengers. Crowded together below deck for up to two months, with stale water and little food, the passengers often became sick and died. Some vessels sailed peacefully across the Atlantic, while others had nothing but trouble. The *Falmouth*, the *Annabella*, the *Alexander* and the *Elizabeth* were four such ships. Thomas Curtis sailed to Prince Edward Island in 1775 aboard the latter vessel, and upon returning to England wrote a long account of his experiences. The following is a paraphrased and abbreviated account of his travels.

THE WRECK OF THE ELIZABETH

In 1775 I was a young man in London, England, looking for a way to make a quick fortune. One day, I learned that Robert Clark was planning to take settlers to St. John's Island and went to visit him. His stories about the Island convinced me to travel to this glorious land. The rivers were filled with fish. There were so many deer and turkeys, he said, you shot them through the window. It all sounded good. You could have offered me £500 to stay in London and I would have refused.

The Elizabeth set sail on August 18, 1775. For three days I was so seasick I didn't leave my bed. For those of us who could not afford rooms on deck, it was very disagreeable. Candles provided our light, pails our washroom, and salt water our bathwater.

After a week or two, our appetites returned. But salted beef and pork, with pudding twice a week, was not my idea of living. It was about this time that we began to drink our sorrows away. There was nothing to do all day but watch the sky and the waves. One day we gave some rum to the sailors. We regretted this afterwards because if the storm had come twelve hours earlier, we would all have been drowned. I mention this as a warning to others.

Several weeks later we sighted Newfoundland. The weather turned very cold. Porpoises surrounded our vessel until we fired several shots at them. That evening we caught our first fish—cod and halibut. They were cooked in a large iron pot with slices of pork fat.

The dish is called chowder. It burnt in the pot, but having had nothing fresh for many weeks, most of us ate so much we were sick afterwards.

On the fifth of November, one of the men on deck cried out "land on the lee bow". The wind was blowing hard and we all feared for our lives as the gale blew us towards shore. The anchors were dropped, but still we drifted closer to the sand banks. The captain ordered the masts cut down. Nothing worked! We could see the terrible breakers we must pass through to arrive safely on shore. The damaged ship drifted over four sand bars before running aground.

The lifeboats were brought out. But no one wished to go first for fear the beach was quicksand. Finally, one brave man volunteered. In a few hours we were all safe on shore. A fire was started to warm our limbs, and we gave thanks to God.

GETTING STARTED

We had nothing; no chair, no table, no bed, no food and no shelter. All that touched my lips for three days were a few cranberries, wet tobacco and salt water. What the others had in their pockets I didn't know, but I did not hear of anyone having more than a few soggy biscuits.

That first evening we decided to gather wood to make a shelter. As we had nothing but pocket knives, the shelter leaked and we spent the night huddled before the fire. I had come ashore with my warm cork jacket and did not take it off night or day. No money in the world could have bought it from me.

The second night the storm blew our house down. It then began to snow. By the morning, everyone was complaining of hunger. I imagined such horrible scenes as eating our dog, or throwing dice to see which one of us would be eaten first. The next morning, however, the wind died down, and we paddled out to the ship. The casks of oatmeal were soggy and full of sand, but everyone was so hungry that we dipped our heads into the barrels. We ate more like pigs than men. Later, the women cooked oatmeal cakes. Although they were burnt on the outside and raw in the middle, the cakes were the sweetest thing I had ever eaten in my life.

For the next week we worked constantly to rescue the clothing and equipment from the vessel. We were constantly wet. When the exhausted men lay down to sleep by the fire, two men kept watch to keep their feet from getting too close to the flames. On the ninth day a boat arrived. We were saved!

■

When we arrived in New London it was so different than I had been led to believe that I began to repent of my voyage and wished myself back in Old London. From the path on our right we could see a little row of log houses and one large house on our left. In all, there were sixteen houses, only one being two storeys. This comprised the whole of the famous New London. We seldom have anything to drink but water, rum being in short supply. For a long while we had nothing to eat but salt fish and potatoes, which we have three times a day, sometimes hot and sometimes cold. The stories about shooting deer and turkey from the windows were evidently deceptions to encourage us to come to this forsaken place.

A ship's passenger list can be an excellent source of information for those who wish to trace their family tree. A partial list for the Elizabeth shows that the following people were on board: James Townsend, farmer, Elizabeth, wife of James, and their children, John, Lucy, Richard and Mary. The family's servant, Thomas Edmonds, also accompanied them aboard ship.

TO STAY OR NOT TO STAY

Provisions were scarce in these early years of British settlement. Only a few villages were self-sufficient. The rest relied on Great Britain for supplies. In the same month that the *Elizabeth* landed on the north shore, two American warships appeared in Charlottetown harbour. The Thirteen Colonies had just declared their independence from Great Britain, and several American privateers were taking advantage of the situation to loot British towns in North America. The acting governor, Phillips Callbeck, wrote the following edited account of this raid:

> We had no soldiers to defend the town.... Despite my kind words, the American captain ordered me aboard his ship. One of the sailors hit me in the face. The invaders then began to loot the town. They broke into the warehouses and stole the food and supplies intended for the settlers. Next, they smashed their way into my house.... Not satisfied with this, these evil men drank our wine. Then they began

to hunt for my wife to 'cut her throat'. This was because her father was living in the United States and was loyal to Britain. Fortunately, Elizabeth was at our farm in the country. These brutal men left us without a single glass of wine, without a candle to burn, bread to eat, nor clothes to wear.

After this cruelty, Mr. Wright, a prominent Charlotte Town citizen, was also captured. The rebels swore and laughed at the tears of his wife and sister. Finally, they sailed away. Mr. Wright and I were forced to go with them.

The affair ended happily for Callbeck and Wright. When the ship landed in Boston, George Washington apologized for their rude treatment and set them free. New London was not as lucky, as the plundered provisions had been intended for the settlers there. The winter that Curtis spent on the Island was thus one of the darkest in its history.

Thomas Curtis' experiences were worse than most of the pioneers, and he returned to England as soon as he could. The final words in his diary were: "I can not express the joy I felt when I arrived home, the 2nd of February, 1777."

PIONEER LIFE

Most British immigrants were not prepared for the Island wilderness. The land had to be cleared of trees, stumps and rocks. Homes had to be built and crops planted before winter. And virtually no one on the Island could advise them. Progress was agonizingly slow. The British government generally ignored P.E.I. in favour of its other North American colonies. The Island lacked rich mineral deposits, and Americans controlled the Gulf fishery. Farmland was inferior to many areas in Nova Scotia, and few settlers wished to rent land on the Island when they could purchase their own farm quite cheaply in other British colonies. As a result, the Island generally attracted only the poorer and less-educated immigrants.

Slowly the population increased, and more and more land was cleared. By 1800, P.E.I. had become self-sufficient in food and began to export small surpluses. Twenty years later, the population had grown to about fifteen thousand people. By the 1830s, the settlers had developed a sense of community and local pride. As one visitor to the Island wrote in 1834, "Verily, this is a good poor man's country!"

The Acadians and the Micmac had the toughest row to hoe. The few Acadians who had escaped deportation lived for several years in fear of being forcibly removed from the Island. They supported themselves by hunting and fishing. Occasionally, British merchants hired them as fishermen or boat-builders, and paid them with clothing, rum, flour and ammunition. As the numbers of British immigrants increased, the Acadians were forced to give up the land they had cleared and travel elsewhere. Some families moved several times. No sooner had they cleared the land than they were evicted by the landlord. Eventually the Acadians made their way to Egmont Bay, Tignish, Miscouche, Mont Carmel, Cascumpeque, Rollo Bay and Bloomfield. In addition, Roman Catholics were not legally allowed to own land until 1786.

Since there were so few Acadians on the Island, and each community was remote from the others, Acadian settlements tended to become inbred. As one missionary wrote to his superior in 1800: "I cannot disapprove of the aversion they have for marrying their neighbours (the English, the Scots or the Irish) because it has meant that they have kept their faith, their customs, and their piety intact." Despite being isolated from each other, the Acadian communities clung to their traditions and resisted assimilation. Physically, they lived apart from the other inhabitants, and even retained traditional costumes which further set them apart. Unfortunately, this isolation meant that the Acadians were slower than other ethnic groups in adopting new agricultural methods.

The other ethnic groups also tended to settle in their own small, isolated coastal communities. The Scots were the largest single

The first two verses in this ballad by Julitte Arsenault describe the departure of one group of Acadians from Malpeque to Egmont Bay.

Who were the ones who drove us here?
Twas the wicked people in our land.
A whole crew they were.
Agin the Acadians
And all together
Living off our goods.
Scarcely do we pick a grain of wheat
When we have to run to them with it.
Those barbarians
Without charity
Care not one bit
For our poverty.

group, but they were divided among themselves by religion and language. Some Highlanders spoke only Gaelic. Roman Catholics, whether Scottish or Acadian, were denied the vote until 1830. Many of the English settlers were merchants and public officials. This group tended to dominate the colony's commercial and political life. The three hundred and eighty Loyalists who came to the Island following the American Revolution were prosperous farmers and merchants who founded several communities, including Bedeque. Many of them, however, soon left when they discovered that there was land for rent but not for sale. Although the Irish did not come in large numbers until the 1840s, by the 1820s many Irish lived in the capital city of Charlottetown.

Regardless of ethnic background, pioneer life was basically the same for everyone. Most work was done by hand. The first ploughs had only one handle. Farmers broadcast seeds by hand, harvested the grain with scythes, gathered it with wooden rakes, and threshed the grain by beating it upon the ground with flails. They then cleaned the grain by tossing it into the air and letting the wind carry off the lighter chaff. The first mechanical threshers, powered by a horse walking on a treadmill, appeared in 1828. As late as 1791, there was only one road on the Island (it joined Covehead and Charlottetown). A trip from the capital to Princetown could take up to two weeks. To solve this problem, the government compelled every male over the age of twenty-one to work eight hours on the roads at least four days each year.

The first settlers had little time to plan their houses, which were usually small log cabins made from newly cut trees. When the land was cleared, they had more time to decide on the type of house they wanted. Of course, the wealthier the family was, the more choices it had. The actual building depended upon the architectural style popular at the time, the building materials available (wood, brick or Island sandstone), the climate, and the ethnic background of the owners. Neighbours frequently joined in house-raising frolics to help new families erect their homes before winter. Food and drink were provided, and everyone stayed after supper for singing and dancing to the sound of the violin. To keep out the cold, the settler filled the spaces between the round logs with moss, mud and wood chips. A large fireplace provided warmth, light and heat for cooking. In winter evenings, the pioneers rolled a back log onto the fire to keep it burning all night. Hot embers, placed in metal containers, served as temporary heating pads.

St. John's Presbyterian Church, Belfast, P.E.I.
was built in 1824 by Selkirk settlers.
Robert Tuck, TIM

Although a great many different types of homes were built on Prince Edward Island in the 1800s, there were several distinctive styles. The most common style of house built between 1830 and 1860 was a storey-and-a-half high and had a small window above the front door. Often a kitchen wing was added to one end.

The farmers left the stumps of the cleared trees in the ground to rot, and planted potatoes around them. The ground appeared to be covered with small mole-hills. The major crops were oats, wheat, barley, flax, peas, turnips and hay. The settlers' diet consisted of oatmeal, porridge, potatoes, pickled herring, cod, wild berries, shellfish, ducks and geese in season. Surplus potatoes and oats were sold in Newfoundland and Nova Scotia, and the money was used to purchase imported tea, tobacco, nails, molasses, rum, sugar and manufactured goods. The settlers made most of their own clothing and furniture. Flannel underwear and linen sheets made from flax were rough and scratchy.

Cash was scarce. Indeed, the first bank on P.E.I. did not open until the 1850s. As a result, bartering was common. A doctor, for example, might be reimbursed for a visit with a barrel of oats, or a freshly killed chicken. Pioneer conditions on P.E.I. attracted few qualified doctors. Those who did come charged high fees. As a result, most people preferred to rely upon home remedies, midwives and lay healers. Although such remedies as inhaling turpentine fumes to cure whooping cough were ineffective and occasionally harmful, doctors' prescriptions were often even more injurious. The medical profession knew nothing about anesthetics, bacteria or sterilization, and surgery was often fatal. Diagnosis was based upon the patient's symptoms, and by the state of the patient's blood, urine, stools, skin colour, temperature, pulse and breathing pattern. Therapy involved altering these symptoms. Bloodletting reduced fevers and rapid pulse rates. Opium calmed nerves. Alcohol raised low spirits and weak heart rates. Charlottetown physician John Mackieson recommended spiced wine and brandy to restore "drooping strength, elevate the animal spirits, and cure exhaustion, faintness, depressions, grief, cramps and gouty spasms of the stomach and bowels."

Few people had time to acquire a formal education. Families needed the children to work in the fields or in the home. Education did not become free until the second half of the 19th century. A few well-to-do Islanders sent their offspring overseas to be educated. Other children made do with what their parents or an educated neighbour could teach them. The few existing schools were small one-room buildings. The teachers were poorly paid and often were chosen more for their ability to keep order than for teaching the "three Rs". The only qualification was a letter from a clergyman attesting to the teacher's moral character. No wonder so many respected members of the community signed their names with an X!

The division of labour based upon sex was not an issue in pioneer times. Men and women did what had to be done. If this meant that females worked in the fields or chased bears away from the gardens, then so it was. Since most work was done in the home, the division of labour between home and the workplace did not arise. (P.E.I. women were not specifically excluded from voting until 1836, although in the 1770's voting regulations mentioned only male Protestants over twenty-one years of age.) The preparation of food and clothing, and the creation of such necessities as soap, medicines and candles, required considerable skill. Even the well-to-do lady was expected to have mastered the domestic arts, and to instruct her servants in these. Although there were marriages of love, practical considerations often took priority. Widowed women were highly valued, and usually remarried relatively quickly.

Labour was also highly valued, and parents were often dependent upon their children's work, especially when cash and hired help were in short supply. In 1820, for example, Walter Johnstone observed the following family situation in his travels through P.E.I.:

> In the morning I was awoke with the sound of whistling, so loud as to be heard through the whole house. I rose in haste to see what was become of the older branches of the family, that a boy should be sitting by the fire amusing himself in this way unadmonished by anyone [on a Sunday].... As I returned in the evening...I found no little giggling and sport going on among the young people.... [The father] now thought proper to make some apology for the light conduct of his children, which he did in the following manner: "We cannot bring up children here with the sober habits you can in Scotland." " Why?" said I. "Because," replied he, "the children here know that their parents are dependent upon them for help as soon as they are fit to do anything; and if their parents will not give them a good deal of their own way, as other children are getting in the neighbourhood, they will go off and leave them altogether destitute.... If my children that are grown up were to leave me, the old woman and myself...could not make a living from our farm, after paying wages for working it."

Making Soap

The women saved fat and grease for making soap. On soap-making day, a big pot was put over an outdoor fireplace. Into the pot went all the fat and grease that had been saved during the year. Lye, made from soaking hardwood ashes in water, was added. When the mixture was thick enough, it was poured into tubs to cool. If hard soap was needed, salt was added to the boiling mixture. When this soap hardened, it was cut into squares.

Making Candles

The pioneers also made their own candles. When a cow was butchered, its fat was melted, or rendered, in a big pot and made into liquid tallow. Then cotton wicks were strung on rods, and the rods were hung on poles resting between the backs of two chairs. The rods were dipped into the melted tallow. They had to be dipped many times before the candles were thick enough to use. Later, candles were made in metal moulds.

The pioneers had a difficult time. The work of clearing land was brutally hard, and everything around them was new and strange. It was not surprising that they often became very discouraged and homesick, or, like Thomas Curtis, returned home. Religion provided the people with comfort. Church services afforded a familiar atmosphere, and the minister offered spiritual strength. Everyone went to church—except when the snow drifts became too high for the horses to break through. Social gatherings often revolved around the church. The following biographies describe two of the more prominent religious figures on Prince Edward Island in these early days.

DONALD MCDONALD (1783–1867)

Donald McDonald, a respected minister of the Church of Scotland, came to the Island in 1826. McDonald had not been here long when he became convinced that God had chosen him as a special messenger to preach to the settlers. He once called himself "the Trumpet of the Lord".

McDonald soon became famous as a preacher. Wherever he spoke, large crowds gathered. There were few church buildings at the time, so he often preached in the open air or in barns. He was such a powerful preacher that people were sometimes so moved by his words that they broke down and cried. Others became so excited that they stood up during the service and swayed back and forth. Singing was an important part of McDonald's ministry. He loved music and wrote the words to many hymns. These hymns are still sung by some Islanders today.

The pioneers loved to listen to Minister McDonald. He told them that God had not forgotten them, and that although they were living in a harsh wilderness, they were still God's children, and that God was watching over them.

Donald McDonald was a man of great energy. He continued to preach to the people for over forty years. During this time he built more than a dozen churches, and gathered about five thousand followers. He was especially fond of children, and it was said that he knew the names of every girl and boy in all his churches.

When McDonald died in 1867, at the age of eighty-four, one of his followers wrote in his diary: "It was the blessing of the Lord to send us such a teacher in this remote place."

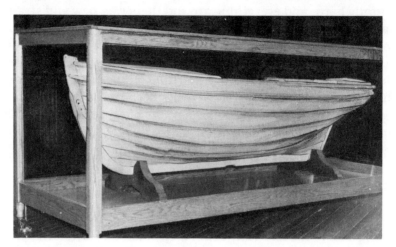

Father MacEachern designed this boat to travel on ice, snow and water. It can be seen in the St. Dunstan's Basilica in Charlottetown.
PEIPA

ANGUS BERNARD MACEACHERN (1759–1835)

Angus Bernard MacEachern is often called the father of Roman Catholicism in Prince Edward Island. When Father MacEachern arrived on the Island in 1790, he faced a difficult task.

Since the deportation of the Acadians in 1758, Roman Catholics had had only one priest in thirty-two years. Angus MacEachern was responsible for the spiritual welfare of Catholics in parts of Nova Scotia, Cape Breton and the Magdalen Islands, as well as on Prince Edward Island. The hardships he endured while travelling from one area to another were almost unbelievable. Without complaint he walked mile after mile through the forests, snowshoed over winter trails, rode horseback through the fields, or drove a two-wheeled gig over rough roads. Voyages by sailing vessels in the summer, or by ice boat in the winter, were taken with little regard for his own personal safety and health.

In addition to looking after the religious needs of his people, Bishop MacEachern also cared for their physical well-being. He was largely responsible for the growth in the number of Catholic churches, from the two that existed on the Island when he arrived, to fifteen in 1835. The Bishop also sought to get the vote for Roman Catholics and helped begin what would become St. Dunstan's College, which later became part of the University of Prince Edward Island.

Bishop MacEachern's presence opened a new era in the history of religion on the Island.

ENTERTAINMENT

The range of entertainment was limited. Everyone enjoyed skating, picnics, horseback riding and frolics. Hunting and fishing provided both enjoyment and fresh meat. Once a week or so the family travelled to the nearest village to sell its produce at the marketplace and buy whatever goods it needed. For a short period, Charlottetown offered plays in a theatre that seated two hundred people. Performances didn't commence until late at night because the actors came to the theatre already dressed and didn't want anyone to see their costumes until the play began. There were several long delays in the show to allow the performers to change costumes, as there were no dressing rooms. The actors changed wherever they could find a room, and the actresses went across the street to the nearest house for costume changes.

Public punishment offered another form of entertainment. Minor crimes were punished by a public whipping, or being placed in a pillory for everyone to see. Theft after dark was a capital crime. The hanging hill on Euston Street between Prince Street and Malpeque Road in Charlottetown always attracted a large crowd. One time, however, the sheriff was unable to persuade anyone to act as the public executioner to hang a woman accused of stealing, and she was freed. Politics were always a lively topic of debate and entertainment.

THE CHARLOTTETOWN MARKET

The Round Market
PEIPA

The Round Market

The first Charlottetown market was a "frame and picket" building constructed in the centre of Queen Square, where Province House now stands. In 1823 the Round Market was built. Butter, eggs and poultry were sold from the centre space. Potatoes, oats, hay, fish, wood and carcasses of beef were sold outside. Market days were Wednesdays and Saturdays.

The M. Butcher Market
PEIPA

The Mark Butcher Market

The Butcher Market House opened in 1867 on a site approximately where the Confederation Centre theatre stands today. It was 45 metres long by 13.5 metres wide. The upper storey was finished as a public hall. The market burned to the ground in 1902.

The W.C. Harris Market
PEIPA

The W.C. Harris Market

The 1904 market was designed by William Critchlow Harris. The second floor was designed and used as a theatre. On April 30, 1958, fire totally destroyed the building. The present Charlottetown market is located on Belvedere Avenue opposite the University of Prince Edward Island.

EIGHT

*Architect's drawing of the Courts of Justice
and Houses of Assembly that were later built in Charlottetown.*
PEIPA

EARLY ISLAND GOVERNMENT

Following the British conquest, the Island was governed by the authorities in Nova Scotia. In 1769, St. John's Island was separated from Nova Scotia, and a governor was appointed to look after the Island's affairs. The governor was the most important political person in the colony. He appointed most of the judges, sheriffs and military officers. He was leader of the armed forces on the Island, and every law required his signature.

The first governor was Captain Walter Patterson, a native of Ireland. He was probably quite shocked when he first stepped ashore in Charlottetown in 1770, since there were only two decent buildings and a few log huts in the entire town, although it was the capital of the Island. There was no courthouse, no jail and no place of worship.

During the first few months, Governor Patterson was kept busy just attending to his everyday needs. A house was built to keep out the approaching cold. Since there was no extra food available on the Island, the governor bought his winter's supply of food and clothing from Nova Scotia before the Northumberland Strait froze. Captain Patterson was expecting more officials to come to the Island that year, but the conditions were so bad in Charlottetown that he warned them not to come until later. "There is not a house to put your head into," he moaned, "and if you do not bring food and other goods to last until June, you will starve because there is not a loaf of bread, or the flour to make a loaf, to be bought on the Island."

Patterson's most important task was to establish a government to make rules and regulations for the Island. He selected seven men to help draw up laws for St. John's Island. The British government had instructed the governor to choose twelve men, but Patterson said he could find no more than seven qualified people. These seven men formed the Council. Its job was to advise the governor. Unfortunately, most of the councillors had been trained as soldiers and knew very little about government.

As the population continued to grow, the British government decided to give Island men a voice in their own government. In 1773, the first elections were held, and eighteen men were elected to help the governor and his council make laws. Voting regulations gave the vote to male Protestants over twenty-one years of age. Until 1853, property qualifications disenfranchised most squatters and labourers.

EARLY ELECTIONS

The elections were usually wild affairs. Until 1787, everyone had to travel to Charlottetown to vote. The polls stayed open several days to allow distant settlers time to vote, and to enable people to cast their ballots in every constituency in which they held property. The people voted by raising their hands, or by yelling out which candidates they wanted to represent them in the government. Voting tended to take place in blocks, as each candidate's supporters took turns controlling the hustings. Elections were one of the few occasions when neighbours got into fights. These battles were often caused by alcohol. Since voting was not a secret, it was easier to bribe the voters. Candidates sometimes offered free liquor to everyone who promised to vote for them. Fights occasionally broke out among supporters of different candidates. Only much later did the secret ballot and laws against drinking on election days end the violence.

EXAMPLES OF EARLY LAWS

A) Bears and Lynx

A reward of fifteen shillings shall be given to every person who shall kill a bear and bring in its snout as proof. A sum of five shillings shall be paid to anyone who shall bring in the snout of a lynx.

B) Slaves

In 1781, a debate arose on the Island about the slaves who had been brought to the colony. Some people argued that all slaves who became Christians should be set free. Others disagreed. The following law was passed by the Assembly:

1. All slaves, whether Negro or half-black, shall remain as slaves whether they convert to Christianity or not.

2. Slaves may only be freed by their owners.

3. The children of female slaves shall belong to their mother's master.

The most infamous election brawl took place near Belfast in 1847. This area consisted of Loyalists, Scottish Protestants and a minority of Irish Roman Catholics. Election violence the previous year caused many people to question the results, and the government called a by-election for March 1. Ethnic, religious and class tensions, however, remained high, and in two separate incidents during the election, mobs of Irish and Scottish tenants attacked each other with clubs, fists and feet. When the electoral officials attempted to assist the victims, they were also beaten. At least three people were killed, and the blood of countless others stained the freshly fallen snow.

The eighteen elected men formed the Assembly. Although it did not become very powerful until the 1850s, the Assembly gave the people a chance to inform the governor of their opinions and needs. The governor, however, did not have to carry out the Assembly's wishes.

Because St. John's Island was a British colony, no bill could become law until it was approved by the British government. The first laws dealt with such issues as building roads and bridges, hunting walrus and preventing crimes. The most important problem, however, was the landlords' refusal to pay their quit rents. The quit rent money was needed to pay the Governor's salary, to erect public buildings and to help run the government. The lack of funds was partly solved in 1777 when Patterson convinced the British government to pay the costs of governing the Island. However, the problem of collecting quit rents remained.

WALTER PATTERSON: THE FIRST GOVERNOR, 1770–1786

Walter Patterson had a difficult task when he arrived on St. John's Island. The colony was almost a total wilderness. The population numbered little more than three hundred and most of the people were Acadians who could not speak English, and whose loyalty was suspect. They had promised to be loyal, but they hadn't had much of a choice. Those Acadians who refused to pledge their loyalty were not allowed to remain on the Island, nor to fish near it.

Patterson was energetic, intelligent and hardworking. Although he wasn't always diplomatic, he appeared to have the Island's best interests at heart. "St. John's Island is my child," he wrote. "I have fostered it at the expense of my fortune and a great part of the prime of my life." His oldest son was called William *St. John* Patterson, after "his" Island.

THE GREAT LAND SWINDLE

Many of the government officials came to the Island hoping to make a fortune. However, very few government jobs paid well. Thus the officials often vied with one another for the best positions. One way to make money was to obtain land. Governor Patterson's desire to own more land on the Island led to his downfall. In 1781, Patterson decided to sell the land of some landlords who had not paid their quit rents. Eleven townships were sold at a public auction. The date of the auction, however, was kept secret. Only Patterson and a few of his friends attended it. The governor personally bought 40,470 hectares at a ridiculously low price.

This auction created a storm. The landlords complained to the British government that they had not been informed of the sale. They also argued that the governor had taken the best land on the Island, and that he had sold the land belonging to many of those people whom he disliked. The landlords initiated a campaign in England to have Patterson removed.

The powerful Stewart and DesBrisay families were particularly angered by the auction. Patterson had taken most of the best land and left them only a few lots. Their dislike of the governor grew to hatred when it was revealed that Patterson had stolen the heart of Peter Stewart's wife while her husband was sick in bed with rheumatism. The Stewarts and the DesBrisays petitioned the British government to remove the governor.

In 1786, Governor Walter Patterson was ordered to return to England, but he refused to comply for another three years. When he finally arrived in Great Britain, Patterson was bankrupt. His property on St. John's Island had been sold by his enemies for much less than it was worth. The British government would not offer him another post. Walter Patterson, the Island's first governor, died in London in 1798, in poverty and disgrace.

*His Royal Highness, Prince Edward, after whom the Island
was named in 1799*
Confederation Centre Library

ANOTHER NAME CHANGE FOR THE ISLAND

Prince Edward Island has had many names, from the Micmac "Abegweit", or "Minegoo", to the French "Île St. Jean", to the British "St. John's Island".

In 1780, the Island government declared that there were at least eight ports, rivers and forts named St. John in the Atlantic colonies. Since the Island was often confused with these locales, and mail was frequently sent to the wrong place, the legislature renamed the Island "New Ireland". This name was probably selected by Governor Patterson, who was a native of Ireland. The British government, however, refused to accept it, arguing that "New Ireland" had already been taken by another colony. "You may," it wrote, "change the name to *New Guernsey* or *New Anglesea.*" These two suggestions were turned down by the Island government.

Finally, in 1799, the colony was officially named Prince Edward Island in honour of the son of King George III. Prince Edward had never visited the colony, but he had ordered that its defences be improved. This is one reason why the Island's government selected him. What the people didn't know was that the Prince had suggested that the government of St. John's Island be joined with the government of Nova Scotia. If this fact had been known, the province probably would not have its present name.

NINE

William Cooper, Island Politician
PEIPA

POLITICS AND THE LAND QUESTION

MURDER AT BAY FORTUNE

According to local legend, one day not too long ago, an old man from Bay Fortune fell asleep in church. When he awoke, the minister was preaching from the Bible about Cain murdering Abel. "You're wrong, sir," said the old man. "It was Pat Pearce who murdered Abell. I can show you the exact spot."

Edward Abell was hired by James Townshend to look after Lot 56, and to collect rent from the ninety tenants who lived there. Abell was a fairly well-to-do farmer and merchant. Part of his job was to evict tenants who did not pay their rent.

In 1819, Patrick Pearce was a tenant on Lot 56. Pearce owned a beautiful black horse that both Abell and his wife coveted. When Pearce refused to sell the horse, Abell demanded that he pay his rent immediately. Pearce paid his rent, but among the rent money were several coins which were good on the Island, but could not be used in Great Britain. Abell refused to accept these coins, and he demanded British money. If he did not get the proper coins, Abell threatened, he would take Pearce's black horse.

As there were no banks on the Island, Pearce went to his neighbours for help. They traded their Spanish coins for his local coins, and Pearce hurried back to his farm. When he arrived, Edward Abell and his servant were leading his horse away. Thinking that he was just in time to save his horse, Pearce offered the Spanish coins to Abell who refused to accept them and demanded even more money. Pearce was furious, but he set off to borrow the money from his friends. When Pearce returned, Abell again refused to accept the payment and the two argued angrily. Abell then sat down on a log to watch his servant tether the horse while Pearce went into his house. Pat Pearce took down his gun, fixed a bayonet on it and stabbed Abell twice before the servant could stop him. Abell crawled into the house, and when the servant went for help, Pearce escaped into the woods.

Abell died four days later. The government offered a large reward for Pearce's capture. Although the reward would have paid the average tenant's rent for four years, his neighbours helped him escape. Pearce was never found, and for a long time his house remained vacant, as many people believed it was haunted.

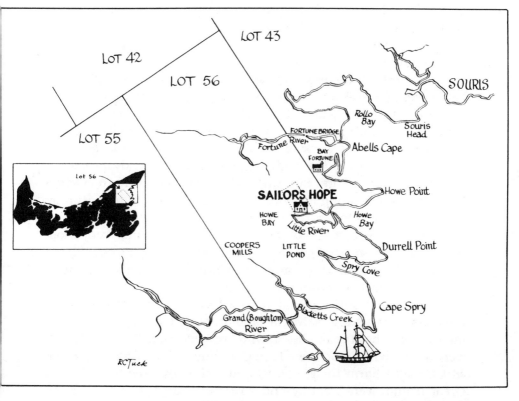

This map shows the location of W. Cooper's home
Robert Tuck

This sensational tale illustrates the land problems that bedeviled Prince Edward Island for over a century, and distinguished Island politics from the political situation in the other British North American colonies. Since few landlords resided on P.E.I., they hired local agents to manage their property and to collect rent from the tenants. Some absentee landlords never made the effort to collect rent, or waited many years before doing so. Other owners had difficulty finding competent and conscientious agents on the Island who would not deceive them. In time, some wealthy Islanders acquired large tracts of land which they rented to the tenants. These land owners were usually no better than the proprietors who lived off-Island.

The standard tenant's farm was one hundred acres, and most leases were for 999 years. The tenants resented putting in years of backbreaking work clearing the land and tilling the soil without ever having the opportunity to own their own land. Worse still, since it took many years of work to produce a farm that could generate enough income to pay the landlord, most tenants quickly fell behind in their rent payments. Since non-payment could lead to eviction (without compensation for improvements), this situation naturally created a sense of insecurity and futility among the tenants. As late as 1860, at least one-half of the recent settlers had apparently lost their land for non-payment. Absentee British landlords considered Islanders to be scoundrels, and the tenants thought of the owners, whether Islanders or absentees, as parasites.

During the first thirty years of the 1800s, several unsuccessful attempts were made to solve the land problem. One reason for these failures was that the landlords who lived on Prince Edward Island were often able to stop the Island government from doing anything which might harm their interests, and the absentee landlords in Great Britain were wealthy and powerful enough to convince the British government to let them keep their land on the Island.

WILLIAM COOPER: THE PEOPLE'S CHAMPION

William Cooper's decision to enter politics in 1830 brought the land question into the limelight. Cooper was born in England about 1786. After spending many years at sea, he settled near Bay Fortune. This was where Edward Abell was murdered by Pat Pearce.

Lord Townshend appointed Cooper to act as his agent. In addition to collecting rent from tenants, Cooper farmed, built ships and erected a mill. Everything went well until Lord Townshend accused Cooper of poor management and fired him.

Cooper switched sides. After working for the landlords, he now became their bitter enemy. In 1831, despite a riot on election day which forced Cooper to hide in a barn, he was elected to the Assembly. Cooper thought that the best way to solve the land question was to establish a special court. This Escheat Court, he stated, would research which landlords had not paid their quit rents to the government, nor settled the required number of people on their land. The government would then confiscate the land of those landlords who had not lived up to their agreement, and sell or give this land to the tenants. The Escheat movement had originated in 1797, but Cooper gave it momentum.

When the British government rejected the idea of an Escheat Court, Cooper organized tenant meetings throughout the Island. He encouraged the tenants not to pay their rents, and created the Escheat Party. Petitions were signed, and rent collectors were threatened by angry groups of tenants armed with pitchforks, stones and other crude weapons. Some rent collectors were hit with frozen cow dung or had the tails of their prize horses cut off. Although some tenants were able to avoid paying rent, many were arrested or evicted from their land. While this was going on, William Cooper paid his own rent and kept his farm, thus enabling his opponents to question Cooper's integrity.

At a meeting of seven hundred angry tenants at Hay River in 1836, Cooper's actions so annoyed the governor that he ordered Cooper to apologize to the government. When he refused, the governor prevented Cooper from sitting in the Assembly. The people, however, showed that they supported Cooper's ideas. In the next election, the Escheat Party won eighteen of twenty-four seats, and gained control of the Assembly. The following year the Assembly sent Cooper to London to convince the British government of the need for an Escheat Court. To save money, he travelled third class aboard a lumber ship. Cooper was given a letter of introduction by the Island's governor. Unknown to him, however, the governor had also written another letter to London which criticized Cooper's character. As a result, the British government would not talk with Cooper. For three months he was put off with delays and excuses.

Cooper finally returned to the Island a defeated man. Great Britain, it seemed, would never accept the idea of an Escheat Court.

Although Cooper was elected again in 1842, many people were tired of his promises—promises that brought no results. In 1849, Cooper and his family sailed to California during the gold rush. Cooper did not stay long, but his family remained. His wife, a daughter and a son died of cholera, and Indians killed three of his remaining sons. Although Cooper remained in the Legislature until 1862, he gradually lost interest in politics and turned to shipbuilding. He died in 1867.

GEORGE COLES AND RESPONSIBLE GOVERNMENT

George Coles and Edward Whelan continued the opposition to the landlords. They were more moderate than Cooper. Instead of using violence and threats to get their way, Coles and Whelan believed that Great Britain would only accept changes if they occurred slowly and gradually.

Coles was born on a farm in Charlottetown Royalty in 1810. After helping his father on the farm for many years, George decided to start his own business. He wasn't well-educated, but through hard work he became a successful manufacturer of beer and liquor. He also owned a steam mill, managed a prosperous farm, and rented houses in Charlottetown. By age thirty-five he was fairly wealthy. He was also an excellent speaker who could quickly spot the weaknesses in his opponents' arguments.

In 1842, George Coles was elected to the Assembly. Coles and Whelan believed that the first step towards solving the land problem was to change the type of government. Island government at this time was largely controlled by the governor. The governor listened to the advice of the Council (which he appointed) and to the Assembly (which was elected), but he did not have to accept their advice. Because the governor had to sign each bill before it became law, he was the most important man on the Island. The Council was next in political importance. It was dominated by a small group of related families (such as the Wrights, Havilands and Palmers) which controlled much of the Island's wealth. All bills passed by the Assembly needed the Council's approval before being sent to the governor.

The governor and the Council were often sympathetic to the landlords, or were landlords themselves. Coles, therefore, believed that the only way the tenants could get a fair deal was to make the Assembly more powerful. He began to push for responsible government, which meant that, in order to remain in office, the Council had to have the support of the Assembly, and that the Council's members would be chosen from the Assembly, much as the Cabinet today is responsible to the elected representatives in the House of Commons. In addition, the governor would be required to sign all bills passed by the Council that concerned purely local matters. If responsible government was granted, the Assembly would have most of the power in the Island government.

The idea of responsible government was not new. Reformers in Nova Scotia, New Brunswick and the other British North American colonies were also struggling to achieve it. Nova Scotia was granted responsible government in 1848. Great Britain, however, thought that the people on Prince Edward Island were too poor and too uneducated to make it work. Finally, in 1851, the Island was given responsible government, and George Coles became the first premier. The governor, however, kept the power to protect the landlords' property rights, and to safeguard the interests of the mother country.

MORE ATTEMPTS AT LAND REFORM

The new government's first attempts to help the tenants failed. Great Britain rejected a proposal to increase the tax on all cultivated land. The Assembly had hoped that this tax would encourage the landlords to sell their land. Great Britain also rejected a bill that would have forced landlords to reimburse evicted tenants for improvements they had made to the land. The Land Purchase Act of 1853 was more successful. This bill allowed the government to buy any estate exceeding one thousand acres, if the landlord was willing to sell. The land was then to be sold to the tenants by the government. In the next seven years the Worrell and Selkirk estates were purchased and resold. By 1873, almost one-third of the Island had been obtained for the tenants.

Progress was being made, but change came slowly. Many landlords refused to sell their estates, and the Island government had little money with which to buy land. Many tenants hoped that Great Britain would lend money to the Island or would force the landlords to sell their land for a fair price. When the British government rejected this solution, the tenants decided to take matters into their own hands.

THE TENANT LEAGUE

Several public meetings in 1864 resulted in the creation of a Tenant League. Each member pledged not to pay his rent and to support other tenants who refused to honour their leases. By depriving the landlords of this revenue, the League hoped to force the proprietors to sell their land at reasonable rates. Although politicians were excluded from the League (as they were perceived to have failed the tenants), membership swelled to about eleven thousand. On March 17, 1865, the Tenant League organized a march through Charlottetown. About five hundred demonstrators crossed the ice on sleighs and horseback from Southport and marched through the city to the accompaniment of a musical band. During this otherwise peaceful demonstration, Deputy Sheriff James Curtis attempted to arrest Sam Fletcher for non-payment of his rent, for which he was two years in arrears. Fletcher knocked the Sheriff to the ground and escaped.

Thus challenged, the government ordered the Sheriff to organize a posse to arrest Fletcher. The posse which assembled on April 7 was a motley group of about one hundred and fifty conscripts who proceeded on horse, foot and in wagons. Some members of the group sang a pro-tenant rights song as they marched along. The expedition took no one by surprise. As the posse marched the eighteen miles to Fletcher's farm, the tenants along the way blew their trumpets to warn Fletcher of its advance. These long horns were normally used to inform workers in the fields that it was dinner-time. During the days of the Tenant League, however, they served to warn the community of the approach of the rent collector.

It was springtime and the clay roads had been reduced to swamps of mud, slush and water. This, plus the political divisions within the posse, did not help the men's spirits. It was Sam Fletcher's tactics, however, that created the most consternation, and exposed the posse to public ridicule. No two stories of the events are identical, but all agree that Fletcher outsmarted the sheriff and his men. At a blacksmith's shop near Vernon River, a crude fort manned with cannons delayed the posse until closer inspection revealed that the fort was constructed of old stove pipes, and the men who manned the guns were only straw scarecrows with paper faces and nightcaps. Later, as the posse approached Fletcher's property, the men were amazed to see Sam calmly leaning against his gatepost, apparently waiting for them. After carefully surrounding him, the men were embarrassed once again. The clothes were Sam's, but the body was straw. Dispirited, the posse returned to Charlottetown without Sam Fletcher.

Edward Whelan, the editor of the *Examiner*, wrote scathingly: "Up to Friday last, Sam Fletcher was an insignificant individual. He is now the hero of the hour; and the ease with which he had turned his back upon the concentrated force of the county...[had] thereby covered it with ridicule." Fletcher had become a popular symbol of successful resistance to authority. The Island government finally sent for the British troops in Halifax to keep control. The disobedience stopped, but the problems remained. Sam Fletcher was never apprehended. Although rumours persisted that Fletcher changed his name and remained on Prince Edward Island, he apparently died off-Island.

When P.E.I. entered Confederation in 1873, the federal government promised the Island $800,000 to help solve the land problems. Two years later, the provincial government passed the compulsory Land Purchase Act. By 1895, the government had bought all the estates, and most of the tenants had become property owners.

TEN

Province House, Charlottetown
Parks Canada

CONFEDERATION

U pper Canadians provided the initiative for Confederation. In 1841, Great Britain united Upper Canada (Ontario) and Lower Canada (Quebec) into the Province of Canada. By the 1860s, however, this union had become unworkable. Many of the Protestant, English-speaking inhabitants of Upper Canada disliked and distrusted the Roman Catholic French Canadians in the eastern half of the province. This feeling was mutual. Unable to achieve a stable majority, the government floundered in indecision, and the economy stagnated. To the south, the United States was engaged in a bloody civil war, and some American politicians were talking about marching north into Canada at war's end.

A few people believed that a union of all the British North American colonies might solve these and other problems. Unity would provide better military defence. A federal union would divide Upper and Lower Canada into separate provinces, each with control over matters of religion and language. A larger country would help the economy. Tariff barriers between provinces would be removed, and interprovincial trade would benefit. In 1864, prominent Canadian politicians John A. Macdonald, George Brown, Alexander Galt and Georges Étienne Cartier joined forces to work towards a federation of all British North America. Their most difficult task would be to convince the Atlantic colonies to enter the union.

The Maritime colonies had briefly discussed the idea of a Maritime Union. Such a merger, some Maritime politicians believed, would turn three relatively weak colonies into a single, more powerful body. The new colony would save money and eliminate such problems as coping with three different currencies and laws. Maritime Union, however, had few supporters. Each province was jealous of its own rights, and only sporadic contact existed among the three provinces. Winter travel was particularly difficult. As one Islander complained about the possibility of sending representatives to government meetings on the mainland: would they be "expected to take pole in hand and leap from iceberg to iceberg across the Straits in the dead of winter?"

Although Prince Edward Island was unenthusiastic about Maritime Union, the government agreed to attend a conference on the topic—but only if the meeting was held on the Island. When the Canadian government learned about this conference, it asked permission to attend and present an alternative proposal. Only then was a date and place set for the meeting—in Charlottetown, September 1, 1864. The course of Canadian history was about to be dramatically changed.

Islanders displayed a general lack of interest in the conference. When the delegates from Nova Scotia and New Brunswick arrived in Charlottetown on August 31, there was no one to meet them. Everyone, it seemed, was at the circus, which was making its first Island appearance in twenty-one years. When the Canadians arrived the next day aboard the steamboat *Queen Victoria*, they received a similar unenthusiastic welcome. Only provincial secretary W.H. Pope was present to greet them. A fisherman rowed him out to the *Queen Victoria* in an old oyster boat with two jars of molasses in the stern and a barrel of flour in the bow. Unperturbed, the Canadians, according to George Brown, "dressed ourselves in correct style," lowered two boats, rowed to shore and "landed like Mr. Christopher Columbus." The delegates met in the richly decorated Province House. The Maritime delegation agreed to postpone discussion of Maritime Union until it had heard the Canadian proposal. Vigorous and reasoned speeches from John A. Macdonald, George Étienne Cartier, Alexander Galt, D'Arcy McGee and George Brown convinced the Maritime representatives that Confederation might be a good idea, and they agreed to meet again in September in Quebec City.

The six days of meetings were accompanied by endless parties. The Canadians had brought along $13,000 worth of champagne to facilitate the discussions, and the Islanders wined and dined the delegates in style. The crowning event was a grand ball at Province House. The library became the refreshment room, and the assembly chamber served as the dance floor. From 10 p.m. until 1 in the morning the delegates and their wives danced to the sounds of two bands. Then dinner was served—beef, ham, salmon, lobsters, oysters, fruits, pastries and wine—followed by three hours of speeches. The next day the delegates left for a tour of the Maritimes before proceeding to Quebec City to hammer out a new constitution.

Thirty-three delegates, including seven members from P.E.I., attended the formal conference at Quebec in October. Once again, alcohol flowed freely as the members and their families partied and danced into the small hours of the morning. Edward Whelan observed that the Canadians seemed to dance every waltz and polka with the wives and daughters of the Maritime delegates, in hopes of

CONFEDERATION TIMELINE

Charlottetown Conference	September 1864
Quebec Conference	October 1864
London Conference	1866
Confederation	1 July 1867
Manitoba enters	1870
British Columbia enters	1871
P.E.I. enters	1873
Alberta and Saskatchewan become provinces	1905
Newfoundland enters	1949

winning them over to the Confederation cause. Constitution-making, however, was serious business, and the P.E.I. delegates were vigilant in protecting provincial interests. It soon became evident that the Canadians did not envision the Island would have much to say regarding national matters. Instead of having provincial equality in the Senate (as in the United States), there was to be regional equality. (The Atlantic provinces, Ontario and Quebec each received the same number of Senators.) In the House of Commons, Islanders sought six seats, but the Canadian delegates insisted on the principle of representation by population, and P.E.I. received only five members for its population of about eighty thousand. The Island delegation also complained about the financial arrangements. Soon the P.E.I. members gained a reputation as obstructionists. When they requested a grant of $800,000 to buy the properties of the landlords, the other delegates rejected the idea. At the conclusion of the Quebec Conference, the Island delegation was divided— Pope, Gray, Haviland and Whelan favoured Confederation, whereas Coles, MacDonald and Palmer opposed it. Most Islanders, however, turned against union and the Island government vetoed Confederation by a combined vote of 36 to 5 in 1865, and 34 to 7 the following year.

OPPOSITION TO CONFEDERATION

Prince Edward Island rejected Confederation for several reasons. Initially, many Islanders had favoured a federal union if advantageous terms could be arranged. However, P.E.I.'s political and economic needs had been largely ignored by the constitution makers. After many years of struggling, the Island was finally prospering, so there was no urgent need to change P.E.I.'s political situation. Shipbuilding and lumbering brought in needed currency. The 1854 reciprocity—or free trade—agreement with the United States had opened new markets for Island farm produce. As a result of this progress, the population had increased from 47,000 in 1841 to 81,000 in 1861. New communities emerged in every part of the Island, and roads linked one end of the province to the other.

Accompanying this economic surge was a growing pride and sense of identity. Although race, religion, politics, and class differences divided Islanders, the Northumberland Strait provided a sense of uniqueness. According to University of Prince Edward Island historian David Weale, Island identity was closely related to the rural nature of the colony. "The habits, the morals, the way of thinking, the temperament, the dialect, the dress, the cuisine, the pastimes, in short, the entire culture and ethos of the Island was thoroughly farm-orientated.... The Islanders, then, shared not only an agricultural vocation, but also a distinct system of values and ideals which grew out of this way of life. The Colony...idealized such qualities as simplicity and frugality; and the residents tended to be extremely suspicious of trends and events in the outside world— particularly in the big cities—which threatened to undermine these basic virtues."

Entry into Confederation would end the province's autonomy and threaten its newly won responsible government, all for becoming an insignificant partner in a larger political unit. The Island, declared one native, would be "like a poor maiden married to a rich gentleman, who priding himself on the superiority of his birth and riches, would not scruple to treat her as a menial servant rather than as a beloved spouse."

How could five representatives in distant Ottawa protect the interests of Prince Edward Islanders? The people thus rejected this and several subsequent offers to join Confederation, including a last-minute promise of funds to purchase the landlords' property.

THE FATHERS
OF CONFEDERATION

**C - Charlottetown,
Q - Quebec**

P.E.I.
J.H. Gray	**C, Q**
E. Palmer	**C, Q**
W.H. Pope	**C, Q**
G. Coles	**C, Q**
A.A. MacDonald	**C, Q**
T.H. Haviland	**Q**
E. Whelan	**Q**

Nova Scotia
C. Tupper	**C, Q**
W.A. Henry	**C, Q**
R.B. Dickey	**C, Q**
J. McCully	**C, Q**
A.G. Archibald	**C, Q**

New Brunswick
S.L. Tilley	**C, Q**
J.M. Johnson	**C, Q**
J.H. Gray	**C, Q**
E. B. Chandler	**C, Q**
W.H. Steeves	**C, Q**
C. Fisher	**Q**
P. Mitchell	**Q**

Canada
J.A. Macdonald	**C, Q**
G.E. Cartier	**C, Q**
A.T. Galt	**C, Q**
G. Brown	**C, Q**
W. McDougall	**C, Q**
T. D'Arcy McGee	**C, Q**
H.L. Langevin	**C, Q**
A. Campbell	**C, Q**
Sir E.P. Taché	**C, Q**
O. Mowat	**Q**
J.C. Chapais	**Q**
J. Cockburn	**Q**

Newfoundland
F.B.T. Carter	**Q**
J.A. Shea	**Q**

P.E.I. ENTERS CONFEDERATION

In 1871, the Island government decided to build a railway spanning the 147 miles from Alberton to Georgetown. Branch lines to Souris and Tignish followed later. It would be the first railway on the Island, and the idea proved very popular. Everyone would prosper— or so many people believed. Construction workers would be needed. Factories would be built, and farmers could transport their crops to the towns more rapidly.

The railway branch lines crisscrossed the Island. Every village wanted to be connected to the main line. The terms of the construction contract established a fixed price per mile, but set no limit on the actual number of miles constructed. The railroad thus wound around the countryside. One-third of the line consisted of curves. The company built an average of one train station every three miles of track. As a result, the railway cost far more than expected, and the provincial debt increased from $250,000 to over $4 million. The lenders wanted their money back, but neither Great Britain nor Island banks would lend the government more money unless P.E.I. agreed to join Confederation.

At this strategic time, Prime Minister John A. Macdonald presented the Island with another offer. Macdonald feared that the Island might fall into American hands and be used as a base from which to attack Canada. P.E.I. was also situated in a strategic location to control the fisheries and from which to smuggle goods to the mainland. Its huge debt, plus promises to help solve the land problems, finally persuaded P.E.I. to enter Confederation on July 1,

BETTER TERMS

- Canada to assume Island's debts and liabilities, and to operate and maintain the railway.
- Debt allowance raised from original $25 per person to $50.
- Canada to maintain efficient and continuous telegraphic and steamship communication with mainland.
- Provincial government to receive $52,000 annually plus $0.80 per person.
- P.E.I. to receive six Members of Parliament. (The population had increased since 1864.)
- The Island would get $800,000 to buy land from the proprietors.

1873. The Island had already adopted the Canadian decimal coinage system. However, as the following statement from the *Patriot* indicates, Confederation was not popular. "At 12 o'clock noon, the Dominion Flag was run up the flag staffs at Government House and the Colonial Building, and a salute of 21 guns was fired from St. George's battery and from H.M.S. *Spartan* now in port. The church and city bells rang out a lively peel.... But among the people who thronged the streets there was no enthusiasm.... After the reading of the Proclamation was concluded, the gentlemen on the balcony gave a cheer, but the three persons below...responded never a word."

ELEVEN

The EMPRESS *on the Montague River*
PEIPA

SHIP AHOY!

The period from 1830 to 1880 is sometimes called the "golden age" of Prince Edward Island. The Island prospered during this time. There were still poor people, but Islanders were generally doing very well. One of the main reasons for this prosperity was the growth of shipbuilding.

The Island was perfectly suited for shipbuilding. All that was needed to set up a shipyard was a sheltered harbour, with a deep body of water at high tide, and a good supply of timber. By the 1830s, shipbuilding yards were scattered over a hundred different locations. Islanders made more money sailing and selling ships than they did exporting their agricultural goods.

Shipbuilders such as Lemuel Cambridge, William Ellis, James Peake, James Yeo, John Douse, James Duncan, William Richards, L.C. Owen, J.C. Pope and William Heard gained a reputation for their well-built vessels. Not every type of sailing ship was built in each port. Shipyards in Mount Stewart concentrated on brigantines; those in Grand River and Port Hill preferred barques and barquentines; and those in Souris and New Glasgow concentrated on schooners. In general, vessels built on Prince Edward Island were smaller than those constructed in either Nova Scotia or New Brunswick.

BUILDING A SHIP

The timber was usually cut in winter and hauled out of the woods by teams of horses or oxen. Some farmers earned extra money in the winters this way. Often, however, landlords had their tenants strip the timber from their land, or forced the tenants to do the work in order to pay their debts. The work of building ships began with the approach of spring. Soon the shipyard was alive with the sound of axes thudding into wood. Saws ripped timber into planks. The planks for the hull of vessels were placed in a steambox to soften them.

The vessel's keel and frame were made mainly from hardwood trees. Juniper and spruce were used for planking the frame and the deck. Pine wood made the best masts and spars. Shipwrights, carpenters, sailmakers, chandlers, blacksmiths, riggers and sparmakers were needed for the construction of a sound vessel. Shipbuilding encouraged the growth of these occupations, which in turn brought prosperity to the nearby villages. Summerside, for example, owed its growth to shipbuilding. By 1871, Summerside had passed Georgetown in importance, and was second in size only to Charlottetown.

THE LAUNCHING

Everyone looked forward to launching day. Schools and stores closed, students and workers took the day off. The vessel to be launched was often gaily decorated with flags. Ladies and gentlemen dressed in their finest clothes. When the shipbuilders began to grease the ways, or slip, the crowd became silent. The tense moment was at hand: would she float? Before the blocks holding back the vessel were knocked out, a bottle of champagne was broken over the hull and the vessel was christened. When the stern hit the water and the boat floated, a great cheer burst from the crowd.

After the launching, many vessels were filled with squared timber and sailed to Great Britain. There, both the timber and the ship were sold. Other vessels were sold in Nova Scotia and New Brunswick. Newfoundland sailors bought schooners and brigantines for sealing and fishing. Some Island shipbuilders kept their vessels and used them to carry potatoes, oats, wheat, lumber, fish and livestock to Newfoundland, Nova Scotia, the United States and the West Indies. Between 1830 and 1873 there were over three thousand such launchings on the Island. The following graph shows the number of new ships registered on the Island.

JAMES YEO (1789–1868)

James Yeo was one of the Island's most successful shipbuilders. He was born with two disadvantages. He had a poker spine, which meant that to bend over, he had to flex at the hips. Despite this problem, Yeo was very strong and had great physical endurance. His second disadvantage was to be born into a poor British family. However, when James Yeo died seventy-nine years later, he was the richest man on Prince Edward Island.

The first thirty years of Yeo's life were filled with unhappiness. His wife, who gave birth to three sons, died in 1818 and Yeo began to drink heavily. Partly as a result of this, his small business failed. The next year his luck changed. James was hired by Thomas Bur-

The AURIGA *was the last barque to be built at New Bideford.*
It is shown here preparing to enter the docks at Bristol, England.
Peabody Museum, Salem

nard to manage his lumber gangs, and to help with Burnard's store and shipbuilding business on P.E.I.

In the next two decades, Yeo combined hard work, intelligence and ruthlessness to make a fortune. When Thomas Burnard died in England, Yeo apparently pretended he was Burnard's agent and collected money from those who were in debt to Burnard. James Yeo used this money to go into business for himself. He became a lumber dealer and a storekeeper in Port Hill, and master of a small schooner. He later pretended to own much of the land in Prince County and, it was said, sent in his own men to cut valuable timber. Because many of the tenants were illiterate and could not read their leases, Yeo was able to get away with this deceit.

The hardworking Yeo rode all over Prince County to supervise his operations. Sometimes his horse trotted on through the night as he slept in the saddle. Yeo had an excellent memory and could quickly calculate crop figures and business statistics in his head. As he became more powerful, Yeo was elected to the government, and was appointed Justice of the Peace. The entire family helped with his businesses. His second wife and their five daughters managed his store at Port Hill. They sold the tobacco, salt, tea, rum, nails, shoes, molasses, meat, cloth, rope and saws that Yeo's ships imported from Great Britain and Nova Scotia. His sons helped buy lumber, oats, livestock and salted cod which were exported to Great Britain in Yeo's ships. His two youngest sons and his sons-in-law built over two hundred vessels. Many of these sailed unfinished to England where they were completed at the family's shipyard, which was managed by Yeo's oldest son, William. With his family's aid, James Yeo became the largest shipbuilder on the Island.

During his life, Yeo was responsible for the construction of about three hundred and fifty vessels, two hundred and fifty of which he sold in Great Britain. The others were used to carry agricultural and lumber goods to Britain, and to return with immigrants and manufactured items not available on the Island. Although he was not a popular man, by the time James Yeo died of pneumonia in 1868, he had done much to develop the Island's economy.

THE END OF THE AGE OF SAIL

Shipbuilding began to decline rapidly after 1875. There were several reasons for the collapse of shipbuilding, the most important of which was a change in world technology. Wood, wind and sails were now being replaced by steel and steam. In addition, the Island had used up most of the trees suitable for large masts. Lumber had to be imported from New Brunswick, which increased the price of the ships. By 1880, the "golden age" of shipbuilding had virtually ended. Many people found themselves without jobs. Because other areas of the economy also were not doing very well, there were few prospects of finding new jobs. As a result, many Islanders left for the United States, especially New England; between 1870 and 1900, approximately thirty thousand Islanders left the province. The prosperous, pre-Confederation days were over.

TWELVE

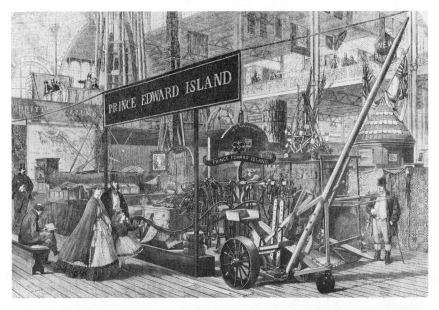

Island industry display at an international exhibition in the 1850s
CCAGM

THE WORKING WORLD
1850–1920

The economy of Prince Edward Island in the 1800s was based on the small family farm. If the farmer prospered, so too did the merchants and manufacturers. Island crops were so plentiful that oats were exported to Great Britain; cattle, sheep, and potatoes went to Newfoundland; potatoes were shipped to Bermuda; and grain, pork and potatoes were sold in Nova Scotia and New Brunswick.

The number of people engaged in fishing also rose during these years. The Island sold dried cod, salt herring, mackerel, gaspereaux and fish oil to the United States. By 1890, Island fishermen realized that profits could also be made from lobster and oyster fishing. Soon, these two seafoods dominated Island fisheries.

Prior to this time, no economical method existed to keep lobsters alive until they reached the market. Unlike cod or mackerel, lobsters could not be dried, salted or pickled. The advent of lobster can-

Fishing craft in Souris in 1910
PAC

ning procedures changed this crustacean from a fertilizer to a delicacy. Between 1873 and 1883, the number of canneries rose dramatically from two to about one hundred, and the value of the Island fishery increased from $218,000 to $2,000,000. Unfortunately, lobster catches soon declined. In 1889, the federal government established two separate lobster fishing seasons, and made it illegal to keep lobsters with the eggs attached. Later, minimum sizes were established and lobster fishermen were licensed. Fortunately, international treaties had always banned Americans from taking lobsters and shellfish from Island waters, and lobster catches remained high. In the 20th century, better traps and such technological changes as gasoline-powered engines, canning methods, refrigeration and faster transportation led to more efficient marketing and processing.

IMPROVED FARMING METHODS

Much of the credit for the growth in agriculture belonged to the many agricultural societies which were organized between 1825 and 1850. These societies encouraged farmers to use modern farming methods. They organized fairs, offered prizes, gave talks, and imported new grains and farming machines. Clydesdale horses; Ayrshire, Shorthorn, Hereford and Angus beef cattle; Leicester sheep; and Yorkshire, Berkshire and Tomworth pigs were imported to improve Island livestock. Farmers began rotating their crops rather than planting the same grain year after year and ruining the soil. Fertilizer was particularly important. Without it, the Island soil soon became exhausted. Fish, lobster shells, barnyard manure and mussel mud were the most widely used fertilizers during this period.

THE MUD DIGGERS

The term *mussel mud* is not quite correct. Although there were mussel shells in the mud, it was the large amount of oyster shells that provided the valuable lime for the soil. In some areas, these mussel mud shell beds were only about a metre deep. More often, they were close to two metres deep, and in places such as St. Peter's Bay, the depth of the shell beds reached ten metres.

Despite its advantages, mussel mud was not used very much until the 1860s because it was too difficult to shovel the mud out of

Growth of Agriculture, 1833-1880

	1833	1880
Acres under cultivation	60,000	467,000
Cattle	30,000	91,000
Sheep	50,000	166,000
Hogs	20,000	40,000
Horses	4,000	13,000

the water. The invention of a horse-powered machine to dig the mud in the winter alleviated this problem. Dressed in warm layers of winter wool, farmers gathered with their sleds near the great wooden mud-diggers to get a load of mussel mud. In such popular sites as North River, South West River, Brudenell and St. Peter's Bay, as many as a hundred farmers huddled together in the cold, waiting to get their sleighload of fertilizer.

In 1916, the government began digging in St. Peter's Bay. The mussel mud was loaded onto railway flatcars and delivered inland to areas which otherwise could not get fertilizer. This "mud special" continued running into the 1920s, but as artificial fertilizers became more available, mussel mud and mud-diggers declined in popularity.

DOING BUSINESS

Agricultural growth also benefited urban areas. Merchants provided the farmers with goods to fill their needs. All types of mills sprang up. There were over five hundred carding, grist, saw, fulling, dressing and shingle mills in 1871. Small factories were erected to manufacture or process goods such as leather, wheels, furniture, shoes, horse-drawn buggies, tobacco, beer, fish oil, bricks, sleighs, clothes, pianos, hay elevators, mowing machines, iron plows and potato hillers. With manufacturing, as with agriculture, the Island was generally self-sufficient. It was during this period that prominent Island businessmen such as R.T. Holman, M.S. Schurman, Malcolm McLeod, J.C. Pope, David Rogers, John L. Mackinnon and John Linkletter got their start.

R.T. HOLMAN (1833-1906)

When his father died in 1846, thirteen-year-old Robert T. Holman left school to take a job in a store in Saint John, New Brunswick. During the next eleven years, he moved from town to town. In 1848, he was a clerk in a Boston drugstore. Two years later he arrived in Charlottetown to work for one of his brothers. From Charlottetown he moved to St. Eleanors and then to Summerside. In each location, Robert was hired by a member of his family. Finally, in 1856, he opened a small store of his own on Water Street in Summerside, where he put his experience and ideas into practice.

Robert had a genius for commerce. His store was always orderly and neat, and he looked after the smallest details. He was also honest. When Robert made a promise, he would rather lose money than break his word. Customers who were unhappy with their goods could either exchange them or get their money back, a benefit few other stores offered.

Holman kept in close touch with the farmers. This helped him decide which goods to buy for his store. Good fortune also helped the growth of his business: a relative in California left him a large amount of money, as did his brother James. In 1857, Holman had only one small store. By 1893, he had a three-storey brick building, a large freight house, a warehouse and sixty employees. Not satisfied with owning the largest department store on the Island, Holman expanded his interests. He built a meat and poultry cannery, began a lobster factory, and became a shipbuilder and owner. When R.T. Holman died in 1906, he had created one of the best family-run businesses in the Maritimes.

FOX FARMING

Although the Island economy began to decline after the 1880s, this was due more to world and national changes than to local problems. The development of fox farming at the turn of the century bolstered Islanders' confidence and brought much-needed money to the province. Charles Dalton and Robert Oulton were two fox farming pioneers on Prince Edward Island.

R. T. HOLMAN LIMITED

Unprecedented Value is the Leading Characteristic of Our Overcoat Department This Season.

Conspicuous in our large stocks is the new and popular Automobile or Prussian Collar Overcoat, of which we have a splendid assortment. Before purchasing your Winter Overcoat be sure to see what we are showing.

A FEW OF OUR BEST ARE AS FOLLOWS:

Men's Plain Grey Heavy Overcoats, full length made from strong Canadian Frieze .... **$ 7.00**

Men's Black Single-breasted Chesterfield Overcoats of good durable Cloth, well made and good appearance **7.50**

Men's Black Shadow Stripe Overcoats, made and trimmed in correct fashion, good looking and serviceable, good value at **9.00**

Men's Fancy Check Tweed Overcoats, smart and nobby and a popular garment.................................... **10.00**

Men's Black and Blue Beaver Overcoats, made with double stitched seams, trimmed and tailored in latest style....... **11.00**

Men's Prussian Collar Overcoats, in a variety of different cloths of plain or fancy pattern, the acme of comfort and the most serviceable garment made,.... **10.00 to 14.00**

Hundreds of other kinds in Plain and Fancy colors, all qualities, from...... .... **5.50 to 18.00**

Workingmen's Jackets

Heavy Frieze Jackets, with belt. **$2.00**

Duck Coats, waterproof and windproof................. **2.50**

Corduroy Coats, Tweed lined... **3.25**

Corduroy and Duck Reversible Coats.................. **3.50**

Heavy Duck Rubberized........ **3.75**

Heavy Duck, heavy lining...... **3.75**

Leather Coats, Tweed lining.... **6.25**

Brown Duck Coats, Sheepskin lined **$4.00**

Brown Duck Coats, Sheepskin lined **5.00**

Brown Duck Coats, Sheepskin lined **5.75**

Corduroy Coats, Sheepskin lined **7.00**

Corduroy Coats, Sheepskin lined **8.00**

Corduroy Coats, Sheepskin lined **8.50**

Corduroy and Leather, Reversible..................... **7.50**

RAILWAY FARES PAID.

From SATURDAY, NOV. 21st, Until SATURDAY, DEC. 5th, Inclusive, we will pay the price of a First Class Return Railway Ticket to each customer whose cash purchase amounts to as many dollars as they live miles from Summerside, viz.: Six miles, $6.00 or over; Twenty-five miles, $25.00 or over; Fifty miles $50.00 or over. Our immense stock of Fall and Winter goods bought for cash in the best markets affords a selection that cannot be had elsewhere and at prices that mean a saving on every purchase.

The Island's Biggest, Best and Busiest Store.

PEIPA

DALTON AND OULTON

In the early 1800s, Charles Dalton was an active young man who loved the outdoors. Much of his time, however, was spent working in his father's store at Tignish. To make extra money, Dalton often went fox hunting with his older friend Robert Oulton. Live red foxes were needed by American hunting clubs for the fox and hound chase. The pelt of the rarer black fox, however, was much more valuable. The guard hairs of the black fox were tipped with silver. The pelts were so beautiful that they were in great demand by the fashion industry. Each man realized that a fortune could be made if black foxes were bred in the same way as farmers breed cows and horses. After several years of working unsuccessfully on their own, Oulton and Dalton decided to work together. They discovered that foxes would not breed unless fox ranches resembled the animals' natural environment.

The two men established a ranch on Cherry Island near Alberton. To make fox kennels, they nailed a board over one end of a hollow log and filled the log with soft, dry seaweed. To prevent the captive foxes from using their sharp teeth and claws to escape into the woods, the men built fences using special wire netting from Montreal. Part of each fence was buried deep in the soil so that foxes couldn't escape by digging under the fence. Male and female foxes were kept separate except at breeding time. Dalton and Oulton also had to learn the animals' diet and habits. The mother fox, for example, killed her young when disturbed during whelping season.

In 1896 their fox breeding practices were finally successful. The fortunes of Dalton and Oulton were now secured. In 1900, for instance, a single pelt was sold in London, England, for $1800. The partners wanted to keep their success a secret. They did not even tell their wives and children about the details of the breeding. They discouraged visitors to the ranch, and hired a guard to protect the grounds at night. So that no one would discover how valuable the business was, Dalton secretly mailed the pelts from a distant post office, or sent them at night by ship.

Secrets are hard to keep. It was not long before other people in West Prince became interested in fox ranching and the wealth it brought. As a result, in 1898, Silas and B.I. Rayner, Robert Tuplin and James Gordon formed a partnership with Oulton and Dalton. The Big Six, as they were called, agreed to keep their fox breeding practices secret and not to produce too many pelts. They knew that if a large number of furs were sold, the price of each pelt would decrease. This monopoly of the silver fox industry was broken when Robert Tuplin sold four fox pups to Robert Holman of Summerside for $10,000. The fox boom had begun. Three years later there were approximately three hundred fox ranches on the Island and the industry was valued at twenty million dollars. The fox boom made some people very rich. Many others lost their life savings.

Fox farming remained profitable until the 1940s. New methods of dyeing, changing fashions, over-production, and the popularity of mink and muskrat furs reduced the demand for silver fox pelts. By 1968, there were only ten fox ranches on the Island. An increase in the price of fox pelts to $600 each in 1976–77 resulted in a renewed interest in fur farming. Since then, prices have fluctuated.

A few reminders of this era in Island life are the distinctive houses built with "fox money". Islanders who had lived in shanties and old homesteads moved into grand houses when they became wealthy by fox farming. Many of these homes were erected by Will Maynard, an architect and builder. The large "fox houses" had balconies, magnificent woodwork and central heating. Although many of the fox houses that were built between 1913 and 1925 are now deserted or broken-down, some of them have been well-kept. They remind us of the brief time when Prince Edward Island was the centre of the world's attention.

THIRTEEN

PEIPA

AN AGE OF CHANGE

About ninety years ago, a young couple was out driving in their horse and buggy when they saw a weird contraption coming towards them. Small explosions and all sorts of rattling noises filled the air. This was the first automobile they had ever seen. The young woman and man had all they could do to control the wild-eyed horses, who reared and bolted in fear. The car sputtered and banged down the middle of the road. Its driver seemingly had no concern for the rights of horses and buggies.

$\mathbf{T}$his story illustrates one of the many changes that took place on Prince Edward Island in the late 19th and early 20th centuries. Not so long ago, streets were unpaved. To light their way at night, city residents carried lanterns. Later, oil-burning lamps were erected at street corners. Electric lights did not come to the streets of Charlottetown until 1887. At this time, there were only eleven telephones on the entire Island. Those people wanting to use the telephone turned a crank on its side and asked an operator to ring the other party.

CROSSING THE STRAIT

The first permanent steamboat connection between the Island and the mainland began in 1842. The boats owned by the P.E.I. Steam Navigation Company visited Pictou, Nova Scotia; Charlottetown; Bedeque; Georgetown; and Miramichi, New Brunswick, every two weeks. However, service was expensive and the boats were never on time.

One of the reasons the Island agreed to Confederation in 1873 was Canada's promise to provide "efficient and continuous communication" between the Island and the mainland. The first ferry provided by the Canadian government was the *Albert* (1875). It was made mostly of wood and couldn't break through the thick winter ice. Although the next steamboat, the *Northern Light* (1876), was steel hulled, it was not strong enough to fight the heavy winter ice, and it averaged only twenty-one round trips a winter. The *Stanley* (1888) was a big improvement. This steel icebreaker was better built and made an average of seventy-nine round trips each winter. Yet even the *Stanley* was subject to the perils of winter. In 1890, for example, it was unable to make the crossing for forty-three consecutive days. The *Minto* (1899) could cut through 28 cm of solid ice; if the ice was thicker than this, the *Minto* was driven onto the ice to crush it with the boat's weight. If the ice did not break, the ship became stranded and the passengers were forced to walk to the nearest shore.

From 1827 to 1918, small ice-boats were used to transport mail across the Strait. An ice boat was usually 5 metres long and 1.2 metres wide, and was covered with tin to protect the boat from the grinding ice. Some of these boats had long metal runners on both sides of the keel. Depending upon the weather, ice-boats used sails, oars or paddles to cross the Strait. When the ice became too thick, the men pulled the boats over the ice on its metal runners. The boat's crew was attached to the ice-boats by long leather harnesses which went over the shoulder and around the waist. The harnesses were used to pull the boat over the ice and snow, and saved the men from drowning if the ice gave way.

The first ice-boats were poorly equipped. After an accident in 1885, in which several men were lost for two days and almost died, each boat was required to carry a compass, two extra paddles, food and the means to make a fire. The men who worked on the ice-boats

CROSSING NORTHUMBERLAND STRAIT BY ICE-BOAT

Prince Edward Island is separated from the mainland by masses of moving ice for nearly five months each year. In 1827, a weekly winter ferry connection was established between Cape Traverse and Cape Tormentine. The boats were sailed, rowed or dragged by the captain, a coxswain, four crew members, and those passengers who wished to pay a reduced fare in exchange for helping.

Crossing the Northumberland Strait from
Cape Tormentine to Cape Traverse
PEIPA

were chosen for their strength and endurance. While those who manned the ice-boats were brave and sturdy, just as brave—or as foolhardy—were early passengers who made the dangerous crossing. The rates were $2 for women; $4 for men who wished to remain in the boat; and $2 for men who helped push or pull the boat across the ice. With luck, a crossing took only three-and-a-half hours. Sometimes, however, the boats became stuck in the ice and the passengers had to walk to shore. In 1843, for example, ten people were lost in the Strait for two days. Twelve years later, two men died during a crossing.

To provide for safer and more regular traffic, some Islanders tried to persuade the Canadian government to build a tunnel under Northumberland Strait. This idea was popular from 1884 to 1914. The first plan was to build an iron tube which would lie on the bottom of the Strait. The enormous amount of money involved, and the complex engineering problems, prevented the construction of such a tunnel. The demand for a tunnel died down after the *Prince Edward Island* (1918) was built. This was the first ferry capable of carrying railway cars and automobiles. In later years, ferries were improved and enlarged. The *Charlottetown* could carry forty-one autos, the *Abegweit*, sixty-nine.

Despite these improvements, ferry service still was—and is—slow. At Wood Islands a private company began ferry services to and from Pictou, Nova Scotia in the 1950s. The idea of constructing a bridge or causeway was discussed in the 1960s. Although a start was made, the idea was abandoned in 1969. Today, as discussed in the last chapter, the issue of whether or not a fixed link should be built is still being debated.

THE AUTOMOBILE

Father George-Antoine Belcourt shocked the people of Rustico in 1866 when he drove a "horseless carriage" to the community's annual picnic. This was the first automobile operated in Canada! Early cars were not very practical. They kept breaking down and were very expensive. By 1907, there were only seven automobiles in the province, but people were curious enough about these new-fangled horseless carriages to pay ten cents for an automobile ride at fairs and picnics, or a dime to take pictures of friends sitting in the front seat.

Islanders not only loved their horses, but also relied on them to transport their produce to market. Horses were often terrified by

REGISTERED MOTOR VEHICLES IN THE MARITIMES
1913–1954

	P.E.I.	N.S.	N.B.
1913	26	511	824
1917	303	5,350	5,251
1920	1,419	12,450	11,196
1924	2,583	20,764	19,975
1928	5,430	35,256	28,072
1930	7,402	43,036	34,833
1933	6,940	40,648	26,867
1936	7,632	46,179	33,402
1940	8,070	57,873	39,000
1945	8,835	56,699	41,577
1950	15,383	94,743	74,415
1954	20,848	133,087	99,058

automobiles, and there were several accidents involving automobiles and horses. Worse, there was speculation that cars would
eventually replace horses. Many Islanders didn't want this to happen, especially since only wealthy people could afford horseless carriages. Some people complained that many farmers stayed home on
market days, and that people didn't attend church for fear of meeting an automobile. In 1908, the government banned automobiles
from Prince Edward Island. The sentence for anyone caught driving
a car was six months in jail or a fine of $500.

In 1913, cars were allowed to operate on Mondays, Wednesdays
and Thursdays, but only on certain roads. Each community decided
whether or not it would permit automobiles. The result was instant
confusion. If a car broke down on Thursday, its owner had to wait
until Monday before driving it home. If an automobile owner lived in
an area which prohibited cars, the owner had to pull the car by
horse to an area which allowed them. Some farmers continued to
object to automobiles and blockaded roads to prevent automobile
traffic.

All restrictive automobile legislation was finally removed in 1918.
Still, it took a while before everyone became used to this form of
transportation. There were many stories about people climbing into
their cars and saying "Giddyup", or yelling "Whoa" when they
wanted to stop. Children amused themselves by writing down the

licence numbers of cars that went by and hurried home to look in car registration books to see where the drivers lived.

Since early cars had no windshields, dust was a problem on un-paved Island roads. Women often wore veils and long coats called "dusters" to protect their clothes. Flat tires were a common occur-rence. The motorist had to take off the tire, remove the inner tube, patch it, push the inner tube back into the tire and then put the tire back on the wheel. Many roads were too narrow to allow cars to pass one another, and a driver might be forced to back up half a mile be-fore there was enough room for another car to pass. The first paved road on the Island was not finished until 1934.

Some early model cars possessed oil lights which had to be lighted by hand, and engines which required cranking. Until 1924, cars drove on the left-hand side of the road. P.E.I. was behind the other provinces in accepting the automobile—in 1921, for example, the Island had one car for every fifty-three people compared to the national average of twenty-eight. By 1931, however, P.E.I. had nar-rowed the gap—in that year, the province had one car for every thir-teen people, whereas the national average was one automobile for every ten people.

An early gas station in Summerside
Allan Rankin

The automobile revolutionized all aspects of Island life. By the 1920s it was no longer a rich man's toy, and had moved from being a luxury to a necessity. The average Canadian selling price dropped from $900 in 1921 to $700 five years later, despite inflation. As car registrations soared, so did road-building, service stations and traffic signs.

AVIATION

The history of flying in Prince Edward Island began in 1912, when a young Cuban pilot flew a homemade plane over the Exhibition Grounds in Charlottetown. But it was not until 1941, when Carl Burke founded Maritime Central Airways, that Prince Edward Island became important in the aviation history of Canada.

Carl Frederick Burke was born in Charlottetown in 1913. When he was a young boy, his greatest dream was to fly a plane. In 1937, his dream came true. While working as a hardware clerk for R.T. Holman, he saved enough money from his $12 weekly salary to take flying lessons for $10 per hour. That same year, Burke bought his first plane, a D.H. Cirrus Moth, and he and his aircraft soon became a familiar sight in Island skies.

In 1939, after earning his commercial pilot's licence, Carl Burke became a pilot with Canadian Airways. During the Second World War, he flew planes from Canada to England. At this time, Burke and his friend, Joe Anderson, made plans to start their own air service for the Maritime provinces. Although Joe Anderson was killed in a plane crash a few months later, Maritime Central Airways of Charlottetown made its first flight in 1941. By 1963, when Carl Burke sold the airline to Eastern Provincial Airways, M.C.A. had become Canada's largest independent cargo airline.

KEITH ROGERS AND RADIO BROADCASTING

Keith S. Rogers, a prominent Island pioneer in the development of radio, was born in Summerside in 1892. He was fascinated by telegraphy and, at the age of fifteen, built his first wireless set in the bathroom of his parents' home. The method of transmitting messages at this time was the "dot dash" or Morse Code system. Keith taught his girlfriend (later his wife) Morse Code and installed a wireless set in her home so that they could communicate whenever they wished. In 1922, there were only fifty to one hundred Island homes with radio receivers. By this time, Rogers was broadcasting noon and evening programs from his living room. Later, working with Walter E. Burke, he broadcast from various locations in Charlottetown.

A group of amateurs, including Walter Burke, Walter Hyndman and Keith Rogers, organized the Radio Club of Charlottetown in 1922. In the spring of 1923, their experimental station 10AS began broadcasting from 3:30 to 4:45 p.m. Three years later, R.T. Holman opened a station—CHGS—in his Summerside store. At this time, Prince Edward Island had two radio stations, New Brunswick had two, and Nova Scotia had only one station. In 1928, Walter Burke opened CHCK in Charlottetown. This station lasted until the start of the Second World War. At the time of his death in 1954, Keith Rogers was planning the first television station on the Island. This project was continued by his son-in-law, R.F. Large, and the first television program was telecast in 1956.

FOURTEEN

Her Heritage/
PEIMHF

WARS, RUM AND THE ECONOMY

T he late 19th and early 20th centuries brought hard economic times for many Islanders. The province had joined Confederation in 1873 to solve its economic problems. However, the advent of steel and steam effectively ended the prosperous shipbuilding industry. Poor forest management decimated the Island's timber reserves, and destructive land use practices reduced farming incomes. Ottawa's adoption of the protective tariff in 1879 aided industrial growth, but raised the prices of manufactured goods, and did little to help agriculture and fishing. The federal government's decision in the 20th century to increase freight rates further slowed economic growth.

OUT-MIGRATION

The most obvious evidence of the hard times was the decline in population, which had gradually increased from 88,000 at Confederation to 109,000 in 1881. Thereafter it steadily declined until it bottomed out at 86,000 in 1924. As the Island's population declined, and immigrants flowed into the Canadian West, P.E.I.'s percentage of Canada's total population fell from 2.5 in 1881 to 1.0 in 1921 and to 0.8 in 1941.

Many Islanders went to Boston, which had commercial ties with P.E.I.. In fact, some wealthy Islanders preferred to shop in Boston rather than in Montreal or Toronto. Although out-migration to the "Boston States" and elsewhere relieved the province of its surplus labour, it tended to be the young, educated people who left the Island. This constant drain of skilled people no doubt had a detrimental effect on subsequent economic development. It certainly resulted in a higher ratio of those over seventy years of age, and placed an increased tax burden on the employed people who remained behind. In 1931, for example, the average age of thirty was the highest in Canada. With no large industries, or forest and mineral wealth to tax, P.E.I. relied heavily on federal subsidies.

THE BOER WAR

The Boer War (1899–1902) and the First World War (1914–1918) temporarily distracted Islanders from their economic woes. Motivated by Imperial sentiments and loyalty to the mother country, thousands of Canadians volunteered to help Great Britain crush the Boers in South Africa. The Laurier government allotted the Island thirty-two men in the first Canadian contingent. So popular was the idea of serving the Empire, or escaping from drudgery and unemployment at home, that Islanders surpassed all other provinces in their enthusiasm to enlist. "There is something stirring and exciting and tingling about it all even here in this quiet little Island thousands of miles from the seat of war," Lucy Maud Montgomery confided to her diary. "Everyone is intensely interested in the news." In all, 7,500 Canadians, including 125 Islanders, served in South Africa. Two Islanders never returned.

Four nurses and one medical officer accompanied the first contingent. The nurses were led by Georgina Fane Pope, a 37-year-old native of Charlottetown, and daughter of W.H. Pope, an Island Father of Confederation. Similar to many other Maritime women, she had attended nursing school in New England before returning to Canada. In South Africa, Pope headed the Canadian Army Nursing Service, and was the first Canadian to be awarded the Royal Red Cross. Two years later, she became the first Nursing Matron of the Canadian Nursing Service. Because of her age, Georgina was denied overseas service in the First World War until 1917. Then, at age 55, she was posted in England and later in France. Shell shock, overwork and constant air raids played on her nerves, and after eight months at the front, Georgina was invalided home. When Georgina Fane Pope died in Charlottetown in 1938, veterans of both the Boer and the First World Wars attended her military funeral.

THE WAR TO END ALL WARS

Several other Island women served as nursing sisters during the First World War. Souris native Rena Maude McLean, for example, saw duty in France and Greece before her hospital ship was torpedoed and sunk on its return to Halifax in 1918. The following year, the Rena McLean Memorial Hospital opened in Charlottetown to care for convalescent veterans.

On the home front, women in every community organized to provide food, clothes and other necessities for the overseas soldiers. Church groups, the Imperial Order of the Daughters of the Empire, the Women's Institutes, the Women's Patriotic Association and the Red Cross Society launched fund-raising activities. They provided relief for prisoners of war, knitted socks, pajamas and underwear, rolled bandages, and helped recruit men for the armed forces. Obliged to tend to the family farm or business alone, many women had to cope with mounting inflation and fuel and food rations, while nervously following the news from the front with its seemingly endless lists of dead soldiers. The impact of the war was inescapable. Skating rinks became shooting ranges, and theatres offered military documentaries to boost home morale.

Overseas, the men distinguished themselves in such battles as Vimy Ridge, Ypres, the Somme and Passchendaele. Many enlisted for the fun and glory of warfare, or for free room and board and a dollar a day, only to find themselves embroiled in four years of muddy and filthy trenches, whistling shells, bloated corpses, rats and lice, poison gas, blood and death. Other men fell victim to volunteer recruiters who scoured the countryside for eligible soldiers to fill the fast-dwindling ranks overseas. "Be a man!" newspaper ads declared, "Get into khaki." Some soldiers, like Harry Leslie of Souris, were decorated for bravery, but more suffered Private William Henry Coffin's fate and were buried quietly overseas. In 1916, the 105th Highland Regiment (one-quarter of its members were "Macs") left for France, singing:

We're from Prince Edward Island,
'Tis a land of noble worth,
You'll see by our geographee
'Tis the only Island on earth.
We have water all around us,
Yet they say that we are "dry";
Oh we're the boys to raise the noise
With our regimental cry.

MAKING THE ISLAND DRY

The war aided the struggle to quell the liquor trade. The temperance movement dated back to P.E.I.'s pioneer days when taverns dotted the countryside. Presbyterian minister Robert Patterson established the first temperance society in 1831 in Centreville. This was followed by the Sons of Temperance, the Independent Order of Good Templars, the Dominion Temperance Alliance, the Women's Christian Temperance Union, as well as Roman Catholic and various Protestant "dry" societies. Temperance organizations combined cultural and educational activities with their evangelizing, and in many rural areas the temperance society constituted the major community organization. The movement had its ups and downs

VOTING ON TEMPERANCE

MUNICIPALITY	YEAR	FOR	AGAINST
Prince County	1878	1,762	271
Kings County	1879	1,076	59
Charlottetown	1879	837	253
Queens County	1880	1,317	99
Prince County	1884	2,939	1,065
Charlottetown	1884	755	715
Charlottetown	1887	689	669
Charlottetown	1891	686	700
Charlottetown	1894	734	712

throughout the century, as "wets" fought "drys" for supremacy. The wets successfully defeated two attempts to pass prohibitory legislation in the late 1850s by arguing for freedom of choice, and by warning voters that taxes would increase if the licensing of liquor taverns was abolished. Lack of success resulted in a change in strategy, and temperance leaders gradually moved from approving moderate use of beers and wine (but not spirits) to total abstinence; and from attempting to win converts by the use of moral arguments, to demanding government legislation prohibiting all alcohol consumption (except that needed for sacramental and medicinal purposes).

The passage of the Canada Temperance Act in 1878 revitalized the Island temperance movement. This federal legislation allowed each municipality to decide by majority vote whether liquor could be sold within its boundaries. It also provided for additional plebiscites every three years if one-quarter of the electorate requested them. As the accompanying chart reveals, Islanders favoured prohibition by a wide majority, with only Charlottetown, the centre of the Island liquor trade, providing opposition. The 1895 federal Royal Commission on the Liquor Traffic thus discovered that Islanders consumed considerably less liquor per person than in any other province. When Charlottetown repealed local prohibition in 1891, the provincial government responded to the resulting increase of liquor-related offences by enacting a law that forced all taverns to have only one door, prohibited them from covering their windows with curtains or screens, allowed no partitions or furniture, and forbade the sale of anything other than liquor on the premises.

Local prohibition, however, did not deter people from drinking. Alcohol passed easily from wet to dry areas, enforcement was weak, and moonshining became both a popular and a lucrative enterprise. (The law did not prohibit the manufacture of alcohol, just its consumption.) As a result, in the late 1890s, a nation-wide campaign began to enforce a total ban on alcohol. In 1898, the Laurier government asked Canadians if they wished a law prohibiting "the importation, manufacture and sale of all alcoholic beverages" for the whole country. Although 51 per cent of Canadians, and 89 per cent of Islanders, voted yes, Laurier did not want to alienate Quebec, which had voted 81 per cent against prohibition, and argued that because only 44 per cent of eligible voters had cast ballots, he was not bound to accept the results of the plebiscite. However, the need for barley and other field crops to feed the Allied soldiers in the First World War, and the desire to create a better world at war's end in which crime, disease and unhappiness would be eradicated, led in 1918 to the federal government's decision to prohibit the import, manufacture and sale of alcoholic beverages in Canada. The United States followed suit with its prohibition legislation in 1920.

RUM RUNNING

The American Prohibition Act forbade the sale, but not the consumption, of alcohol. Since the Canadian legislation ended in 1919, and provincial laws did not prohibit the manufacture of liquor for export, the spirits trade to the United States provided an alternative source of income for the depressed Maritime fishing industry. Hundreds of fishing vessels, such as the famous *Nellie J. Banks*, were refitted and used to quench American thirst. During the 1920s, every province but P.E.I. abandoned prohibition in favour of government-operated liquor stores. Not until 1948 could Islanders purchase a legal alcoholic beverage. However, this situation merely provided another market for the rum runners when the United States ended prohibition in 1933.

In the game of wits between the authorities and the rum runners, the latter usually won. Anchored outside the three-mile limit, the rum runners lured government patrols away through various stratagems and landed their illegal cargo in one of the many deserted bays or coves. Other tactics involved hiding liquor in lobster traps, or attaching the illicit goods to buoys. To help combat this trade, and to control the growing automobile traffic, the province created its own Provincial Police force in 1930. This small contingent in khaki or navy blue uniforms patrolled rural areas, enforced the Lord's Day Act and deported hoboes to New Brunswick, but were generally unsuccessful in enforcing the less-than-popular liquor laws. The growth of rum-running gangs, speakeasies, bootleggers and moonshiners contributed to the Liberal party's defeat in 1931. And the following year the Royal Canadian Mounted Police replaced the provincial police force. Rum running did not end until the government rescinded prohibition in 1948. Bootlegging and moonshining, however, remain as a remnant of this era.

A NEW WORLD

When the soldiers returned from the First World War there were plenty of surprises for them. Automobiles now carefully manoeuvered their way around the ruts in the clay streets. Women voted in federal elections and worked in a greater variety of jobs. Alcoholic beverages were more difficult to obtain, and income tax was now a way of life. More serious was the high inflation rate, an onslaught of Spanish Flu, which claimed as many Canadian lives as had the war, and the growing unemployment as war industries shut down.

The gradual decline of the Maritime economy in the first three decades of the century produced a Maritime Rights Movement. Its proponents sought to use regional co-operation to force the federal government to respond to the area's economic problems. In particular, they sought lower tariffs, larger federal subsidies and reduced freight rates—which had increased by as much as two hundred per cent following the war. Prince Edward Island was less affected by the regional economic malaise than were Nova Scotia and New Brunswick. As a result, Maritime Rights never became a major political issue, and the Island was "bought off" by a Royal Commission and offers of larger federal subsidies and a new car ferry.

FIFTEEN

The smallest chartered bank in Canada
PEIPA

DEPRESSION, SECOND WORLD WAR AND CO-OPERATIVES

Despite the prevailing view that the Maritimes survived the Great Depression of the 1930s with fewer problems than the rest of Canada, the area was particularly hard hit. Although the Island did not experience the perils of drought and grasshoppers which destroyed western Canadian crops, the precipitous fall in farm and fish prices nonetheless brought ruin to many families. Letters written to Prime Minister R.B. Bennett requesting financial aid described animals slowly starving to death in their stalls for lack of feed, children suffering from malnutrition, and as much as twenty per cent of the labour force unemployed. Although prices for farm produce began to improve in 1936, many farmers had no money left for seeds and the land had deteriorated. To make matters worse, the cost of farm machinery and manufactured goods increased at a much faster rate than did agricultural prices.

Destitution was particularly evident in Charlottetown. Rural families could at least feed themselves. As the 1947 Canada Packers strike later illustrated, neither the provincial government nor the majority of the populace had much sympathy for industrial workers. Throughout the 1930s, P.E.I. was the only province that had no legislation regarding hours of work, minimum wage, factory inspection for health and safety conditions, workers' compensation, and (with Ontario) did not recognize the workers' rights to collective bargaining.

The following statistics indicate the extent of the depression. The cost of eggs declined from 30 cents a dozen to just 8 cents. Cod sold for less than one cent a pound and lobsters for 4 cents. Silver fox pelts dropped from $100 to $28. Swine declined from 16 cents to 3 cents a pound. And the price of potatoes, which also suffered from a British embargo on Canadian potatoes for fear of contamination from the Colorado Beetle, sank from $1.50 to 6 cents for one hundred pounds. Agricultural income thus decreased from $9.8 million in 1927 to $2.3 million five years later. The Island's $146 average income per person in 1932 was the lowest in the country. The Canadian average income was $287, almost double P.E.I.'s total.

The scramble to catch skunks indicated the seriousness of the situation. Prior to the depression, a New Annan firm had sought to raise skunks for their pelts. When the public showed no interest, the farm set the forty animals free. However, the skunks adapted so well to the Island that the government offered a 50 cent bounty per snout in order to control their swelling numbers. During the de-

COST OF FOOD IN CHARLOTTETOWN

DECEMBER 1933

COMMODITY	WEIGHT	PRICE (cents)
SIRLOIN	1 lb	22.0
BACON	2 lb	26.0
BUTTER	3 lb	48.0
BREAD	15 lb	100.0
SUGAR	4 lb	30.4
CHEESE	2 lb	38.4
CHUCK ROAST	2 lb	34.6
MILK	6 qt	5.0
EGGS	1 dz	42.3
FLOUR	10 lb	32.7
RICE	2 lb	14.8
POTATOES	2 pk	32.0

pression, skunks were eagerly sought, and some people apparently bootlegged snouts from the mainland. One imaginative person manufactured snouts from cow hide. Within three years, the government had paid bounties on over fifteen thousand skunk snouts.

PUBLIC RELIEF

The provincial Conservative Party was one of the first casualties of the hard times. Although the depression was no one's fault, the Liberals under Walter Lea swept all thirty seats in the 1935 election—a Canadian first. However, neither party varied much in its approach to the problem. With limited financial resources, the government was reluctant to adopt social welfare policies, and P.E.I. was one of the last provinces to provide old age pensions and mother's allowance. In 1933, P.E.I. bowed to public pressures and paid old age pensions to those seventy years of age or over. It set the maximum pension at $15, established a strict means test, and made it mandatory for children to support their parents. Because federal relief programs were administered on a matching grants formula, P.E.I. received less money per capita than the wealthier provinces. University of New Brunswick historian E.R. Forbes has speculated that this shortfall in relief funds hindered Maritime industrial development.

Public works programs were more attractive. The unemployed built bridges and wharves, paved the Trans-Canada Highway and remodelled public buildings. In Summerside, for example, workers constructed a sea wall and a municipal airport, paved the streets, and improved the water and sewage systems. As a result of such activities, the provincial government expanded its bureaucracy and was forced by the circumstances to take responsibility for the welfare of the people.

The 1930s were not entirely without their good times. Many people fondly remember this period for its camaraderie, as communities co-operated to help the needy. Parties held at a poor person's home broke up early, leaving enough left-over food for the rest of the week. "Bees" provided entertainment and financed such useful tasks as haying and ploughing. To help the drought-stricken western Canadian farmers, Islanders sent sixty box-car loads of agricultural produce. This act of generosity, declared one relief official, should be "chronicled as one of the most inspirational gestures in Canadian history. Certainly, if Canadianism means anything, this means a great deal in the shaping of a true and loyal national consciousness."

CO-OPERATIVES

When American professor John T. Croteau drove into the village of North Rustico in 1933, he found it "sunken in misery—a collection of unpainted fishermen's shacks, a falling-down, cold school building, so old that no one remembered when it had been built, and a little mission church. Incomes were below subsistence level. During the winter months many families existed on one or two scanty meals a day.... It was a picture of misery and despair." When Croteau returned twelve years later, he observed that the community was now prosperous thanks to the activities of the resident pastor. "Study clubs were organized. A credit union was formed. A fishermen's union was incorporated and a co-operative lobster factory built. Later a co-operative store was started. As conditions improved the people of the community bought an unused warehouse, hauled it to a new site and converted it into a modern school.... There is a library in the building and radios in every classroom.... The church was extended to more than twice the size of the old one. A paved road was built through the village and electric lights extended through the town."

Co-operative ventures were not new on the Island. Father George-Antoine Belcourt created the Farmers' Bank of Rustico in 1864, and later established grain banks to loan seeds to Acadian farmers. Across the province, farmers formed co-operatives to process and market their goods. By 1931, the Prince Edward Island Co-operative Egg and Poultry Association had 3,800 members. The Potato Growers' Association helped purchase fertilizers, standardize grades, eradicate disease and market farmers' crops. Tignish fishermen organized their own union in 1923, and two years later began operating a lobster cannery. Such ventures quickly multiplied during the depression. The spark behind their growth was provided by Dr. Moses Coady of St. Francis Xavier University in Nova Scotia. Coady was the founder of the Antigonish Movement, which sought to make common people "masters of their own destiny." Copying his methods, Islanders formed credit unions and co-operative stores, and established marketing and warehousing organizations. Coady was also interested in adult education, and, in 1933, Croteau applied the Antigonish adult education program to P.E.I. Working with the St. Dunstan's University Extension Service, Croteau helped form study groups throughout the province. They raised money and provided entertainment by sponsoring dances, card games and socials; examined the major economic problems of the day; and taught the people how to organize and operate credit unions, co-operative stores, unions and community projects. Tignish led the way. Co-operative ventures provided health care, financial loans, groceries, automobile service, fish processing, and marketing services for Irish Moss, blueberries and other produce. Although the co-operative movement declined in the 1950s, it still remains strong in western Prince County.

WAR AGAIN

The Second World War was a time of tragedy. Over fifty million humans died, including 42,000 Canadians. Almost 9,000 Islanders volunteered for overseas service, which was the highest provincial ratio in the country.

The war ended the depression. By 1941 there were enough jobs for all who wanted them, and the demand had increased for agricultural and fishing products. Lobster and fish prices skyrocketed. Hake and mackerel, rich in proteins, were canned and sold to an international agency which supplied food to victims of the war. The

CONVENIENCES IN 1941

PERCENTAGE OF HOMES WITH:

	RADIO	PHONE	ELECTRIC VACUUM	CAR
P.E.I.	60	22	6	29
N.S.	73	33	16	28
N.B.	65	27	12	26
CANADA	78	40	24	37

PERCENTAGE OF FARM HOMES WITH:

	ELECTRIC LIGHTING	RUNNING WATER	FLUSH TOILET	BATHTUB
P.E.I.	6	9	6	7
N.S.	26	14	9	10
N.B.	19	13	8	7
CANADA	20	12	9	7

loss of the Japanese supply of agar, after Pearl Harbor in 1941, led to the collection of Irish Moss for use as a food additive and gelling product.

The threat of invasion from the skies led to a series of practice blackouts during which all indoor lights were shielded from outside view. Over forty air raid sirens were erected in various centres across the Island. Naval attacks, however, were more likely to occur. In May of 1942, a German submarine torpedoed a British steamer near Anticosti Island in the Gulf of St. Lawrence. Later that year, the H.M.C.S. *Charlottetown* was torpedoed, struck a reef and sunk off the Nova Scotia coast. The following year, the Newfoundland ferry, the *Caribou*, went down in the Gulf of St. Lawrence.

When Prime Minister W.L.M. King agreed to take part in the British Commonwealth Air Training Program for Allied pilots, Canada had to select suitable sites. Fortunately for P.E.I., Canada's Minister of Defence, R.L. Ralston, had lost his bid for election in 1935. In desperation, Ralston persuaded the Prince County Liberal Association to allow him to run there in a by-election. The victorious Ralston rewarded his adopted constituency with military bases at Mount Pleasant, Wellington and St. Eleanors. These bases created immediate prosperity in Prince County. The Mount Pleasant base became an air gunnery school. Here, the men practiced shooting ink-coloured bullets at a white silk target pulled behind an aircraft. Although the training school employed a large civilian staff, and was of major economic and social importance to western Prince County, Ottawa closed the airport at the conclusion of the war. A similar fate befell the emergency landing strip at Wellington, the search and rescue station at Alberton South, and the radar base at Tignish.

The St. Eleanors base, which served as a flying school and later as a reconnaissance school, remained after the war and quickly assumed a vital economic position in the area. Local Summerside merchants found a ready market for their goods at the base, and civilians secured employment there. After P.E.I. successfully resisted two threats in the 1960s and 1970s to close the base, the federal government (which lost all four Island seats in the 1988 election) announced that CFB Summerside would be shut down permanently in 1992. Since CFB Summerside was the second largest employer on P.E.I., and annually pumped about $50 million into the economy—Summerside, the second-largest town in the province—faced difficult economic decisions.

SIXTEEN

School at Canoe Cove, Robert Harris
HC/CCAGM

THE THREE R's

Only a few people received a formal education during the pioneer period on Prince Edward Island. The children of wealthy parents were either sent to boarding schools off the Island, or private tutors were hired to instruct them. Poor families could not afford such luxuries. Because the settlers needed all the help they could get to perform needed chores around the farm, they kept their children at home.

In 1825, the government provided a small amount of money for each district to build a school and hire a teacher. The teachers' salaries were so low that some teachers were forced to "board around". This meant that each week the teacher lived with a different family in the district. Conditions were difficult. Most schoolhouses were built of logs. Sometimes forty or fifty children from five to sixteen years of age crowded into one room. In summer, the building was too hot. In winter, if the school ran out of logs for the woodstove, it became so cold that classes were cancelled for the day.

Older students helped younger ones with their reading, writing and arithmetic. In many schools there were no history books, maps or atlases. The Bible was often the only reading book available. Only one school on the Island had a library. Because of these terrible conditions, and the low salaries, good teachers were scarce. Some schools closed because no teachers were available. Teachers had little training and were often hired because they were strong enough to control the older boys. One punishment was called "the peg". Pegs were placed in the wall and when students misbehaved their hair was pegged to the wall, just high enough to keep the wrong-doers on tiptoe.

Another problem was absenteeism, as parents often kept their children at home to help work on the farm. In 1839, the government tried to solve this problem by arranging school vacations during planting and harvesting time—ten days in May and eleven days in October. Students attended classes in the winter from ten in the morning until three in the afternoon, and from nine to four in the summer. Monday through Friday, as well as every second Saturday, were school days. Despite these changes, poor families could not afford schooling. As a result, many people could neither read nor write and had to make an "X" for their signature. Few girls attended secondary school.

The situation improved after 1852. In that year the government passed the Free Education Act which enabled all children over five years of age to attend school, no matter how poor their parents were. A Board of Education was created to ensure that teachers were qualified. There were three vacations—one week in June, one week in October, and from December 24 to January 6. The number of children who went to school doubled within two years. A few years later a "Normal School" was built to train teachers.

Unfortunately, religious differences plagued Island educational and political authorities for the next two decades. Should the Bible be authorized for use in public schools? And should Roman Catholic schools receive public funds? These were serious questions for a society that fined individuals for cutting firewood on Sunday, and was almost equally divided between Protestants (fifty-five per cent) and Roman Catholics (forty-five per cent). These issues vexed politicians from the 1850s until 1877, when the government decreed that all public schools be non-sectarian. Teachers were permitted to open school with Scripture readings (without comments), but student attendance was optional. A series of compromises later recognized that in urban areas, specific schools would be either Protestant or Catholic, and where having two schools was not economical, teachers would be alternated along religious lines.

Despite their size and inadequate accommodations, the little white schoolhouses which dotted the countryside in 1900 had many advantages. Parents and teachers were seldom more than a few doors apart. Everyone helped. The values of the school and the community were therefore similar. Along with the church and the general store, the school was at the centre of each community.

The following memories of Mrs. William "Effie" Campbell describe the joys of school life.

■

In 1909, at age seven, I began in Southwest Lot 16 with about forty other pupils. It was a one-room school with a potbelly stove for heat in the winter. It burned coal and wood. We had to haul the ashes from this stove to a pile out behind the school.

Each day it was a different student's job to carry a pail of drinking water to the school. There was no plumbing and no electricity. At night when we had concerts, we used lanterns, otherwise we just worked by the natural sunlight streaming in through the windows.

Every Friday we were allowed to use our copybooks. These books had printing on the top of each page, and we used pens dipped in ink to copy this printing in the space below. The slates we could take home but the copybooks and the pens and ink were kept up at the teacher's desk. There were also cloths for wiping off the slates. We used to chuck these cloths at each other when the teacher wasn't in the room, but somehow she always seemed to know what we were doing and who was doing it. Then one of the boys, Freeman Campbell, figured it out—she was peeking in through the keyhole in the door. So Freeman took his pocket knife and made a plug for the keyhole. It worked and she never could see what was going on after that.

For punishment we either stood in the corner or had a switch cut from a tree laid on our hands. Most of the teachers were kind-hearted and seldom used the switch, but one teacher used to switch our hands till they were blistered and bleeding and she'd have every kid crying because we didn't know our grammar. But most of the teachers were kind.

■

MODERN SCHOOLS

As the years passed, many of these wooden schoolhouses became inadequate. Lighting, heating, sanitation, ventilation and plumbing were old-fashioned. Few buildings had libraries, gymnasiums, art or music rooms. In 1920, a school inspector wrote that many schools were so poorly built that farmers would hesitate to winter their animals in them. In addition, the poorer areas of the province could not afford to pay their teachers very much. As a result, the best teachers went to the richer school districts, or left the profession.

In 1962, the average teacher's salary in the province was $2700, compared to $4500 in Canada as a whole. Fewer than one out of every ten teachers had completed university. Another problem was the lack of high schools. Until the 1930s, students had to travel to Charlottetown to take grades eleven and twelve.

The response to these problems was consolidation. Instead of continuing to use the Island's many small schools, a few larger schools were built. These new schools had libraries, gymnasiums and modern facilities. The number of one-room schools was reduced from 470 in 1960, to 57 in 1972. In step with the rest of Canada, teachers' salaries and their level of education improved. More students now went beyond grade eight education. A disadvantage of school consolidation was that many children now had to be bused to school and the community was often separated from the school system.

HIGHER EDUCATION

Higher education began in Prince Edward Island during the 1830s with the establishment of the non-sectarian Central Academy and the Roman Catholic St. Andrew's. Later, as the Prince of Wales College and St. Dunstan's College, the two institutions developed different educational philosophies. Prince of Wales College dedicated its efforts to producing students trained in the classics, and emphasized high academic standards. St. Dunstan's combined Christian ideals with social action, and extended its activities into the community. During the 1960s, the provincial government wrestled with the contentious subject of university amalgamation. Various groups supported either separate universities, amalgamation, or closer co-operation. The major debate was between the supporters of a single public institution, who believed it would help end denominational strife and religious intolerance on the Island, and the proponents of the status quo, who preferred to maintain the two distinctive educational philosophies which had become a part of the Island's cultural heritage. In 1969, the provincial government united the two colleges into the non-denominational University of Prince Edward Island, which moved into St. Dunstan's buildings on its present site. The student population at U.P.E.I. has continued to increase, reaching about 2,400 students in 1990.

Holland College began on the Prince of Wales campus in downtown Charlottetown in 1969 with no traditions, but soon created a distinctive role for itself by offering training in practical, job-oriented subjects. It now has campuses in several areas throughout the Island, and operates the provincial vocational high school program, the Atlantic Police Academy, the Culinary Institute of Canada, vocational trade training and adult night classes.

SEVENTEEN

*ANNE OF GREEN GABLES is performed at the
Confederation Centre of the Arts each summer.*
Gord Johnston Photography

ENTERTAINMENT

In the 19th century, each community provided its own entertainment. Strawberry festivals, basket socials, ice-cream parties and special speakers, often combined with such serious matters as political meetings and charity fund raising. Such events were usually accompanied by the local band. In 1890, for example, the Souris Benevolent Irish Society held a fund-raising Tea Party, which promised good meals, games, bowling, swings, hurdles, races, a slippery walk and a lecture by Professor Shuttleworth on scientific farming.

MUSIC

In the evening, the early settlers sang and danced to the music of the bagpipes, fiddle, mouth organ, accordion or jew's harp. At first, music-making consisted mostly of singing or fiddling, since there were usually very few other instruments. Some religious denominations also considered the fiddle a tool of the devil. Most communities had their own church choirs. Music-makers were especially appreciated members of a community. Two of the Island's best-known song-writers were Lawrence Doyle and Larry Gorman.

LAWRENCE DOYLE

Lawrence Doyle was born near Fortune Pond in 1847. When Lawrence was a teenager, his father died and he was left to help his mother and two sisters with the family farm. Lawrence stopped school after grade six. Through hard work and intelligence he became a prosperous farmer. He was also a good carpenter, an active churchman, a school trustee, a postmaster and an amateur veterinarian. It was his song-making talent, however, that made him well-known. One old-timer recounted how Doyle used to compose new songs:

> He was a farmer, but in the wintertime he'd work in the shop making frames, windows and doors. My father was there; he boarded there, and he taught in the school. He'd be in the shop with Lawrence on Saturdays hanging around talking to him, and watching. He said you'd see a smile appearing on his face, you know, and then he'd walk over and take his pencil; he had a little book on his workbench, and he'd write some. Then he'd go back and be working away and by and by you'd see him smiling again and then he'd go and write a little more. And he was making up a song all the time, you know. And that's the way he used to work.

The songs that people such as Doyle and Gorman wrote tell us a great deal about their lives, their communities and the times in which they lived. The song "Prince Edward Isle Adieu," for example, provides a glimpse of Island history.

During the mid-1800s, orchestras and brass bands became popular. Before the invention of radio and television, bands, fiddle contests and step-dancing competitions were some of the most popular forms of entertainment. During the 20th century, music remains popular. People enjoy a wide range of music—classical, jazz, swing, blues, folk, traditional, rock and roll, punk, new wave and many others. Traditional Highland dancing, fiddling, square dancing and ceilidhs still survive and continue to be very popular. A few well-known Island musicians are Angèle Arsenault of Abram's Village, Stompin' Tom Connors of Skinners' Pond, Lennie Gallant of South Rustico, Gene McLelland and Nancy White.

PRINCE EDWARD ISLE, ADIEU

☐

Come all ye hardy sons of toil,
pray lend an ear to me.
'Til I relate the stressful state
of this our country.
I will not pause to name the cause,
but keep it close in view.
Our comrades dear have got to leave
and bid this Isle adieu.

There is a band within this land
We live in pomp and pride;
To swell their store they rob the poor;
On pleasures' wings they ride.
With dishes fine their tables shine,
They live in princely style.
Those are the knaves who made us slaves
And sold Prince Edward Isle.

Each settler must pay rent.
So now you see the turning tide
That drove us to exile
Begin again to cross the main
And leave Prince Edward Isle.
The place was new, the roads were few
The people lived content;
The landlords came, their fields to claim,

But changes great have come of late
And brought some curious things;
Dominion men have brought us in,
With our own railway rings.
There's maps and charts and towns apart
And tramps of every style;
There's doctors mute and lawyers cute
Upon Prince Edward Isle.

So here's success to all who press
The question of Free Trade.
Join hand in hand, our cause is grand,
They're plainly in the shade.
The mainland route, the world throughout,
Take courage now, stand true,
My verse is run, my song is done,
Prince Edward Island, adieu.

LITERATURE

The Island has produced several writers who have become famous. Lucy Maud Montgomery and Sir Andrew Macphail wrote about rural Prince Edward Island. Island poets such as the late Milton Acorn and Elaine Harrison have expressed their ideas about life in poetic form. Elaine Harrison has been involved in Island culture and life for over thirty years. She taught English in Island schools, has published books, painted and written about the Island. *I am an Island that Dreams* has been set to music by Jitky Snizkove, a Czechoslovakian composer, and performed in Prague. This poem was also the basis of a CBC production, "This Land".

Theatre has traditionally been a popular form of entertainment for Islanders. Early in this century, many touring companies brought their productions to eager Island audiences. In rural areas, plays and concerts were popular community events.

In 1964, the Confederation Centre of the Arts opened in Charlottetown. One of its first productions was a musical version of Lucy Maud Montgomery's famous Island story, *Anne of Green Gables*. This endearing show has played each summer at the Charlottetown Festival and on national tours, as well as in centres outside Canada. Other summer theatres include the King's Playhouse in Georgetown (rebuilt in 1984 after fire destroyed the original Victorian-style structure) and the Victoria Playhouse. French-language theatre is presented each summer at the Acadian Village at Mont-Carmel. Lively productions are also staged at the University of Prince Edward Island. The Community Schools movement promotes drama, and Theatre Prince Edward Island assists both school and community groups.

Poet, Milton Acorn
Ragweed Press

ART

The best-known Island artist is Robert Harris. His most famous painting is the study of the Fathers of Confederation, which was used on Canadian postage stamps, on Canadian National Railway dining car menus, and has been reproduced for classrooms across the country.

Harris studied art in England, Boston and Paris, where he became an expert portrait painter. In 1879, Harris decided to devote his life to art. As his fame spread throughout Canada, Harris was invited to Montreal and Ottawa to paint portraits of the country's leading politicians and businessmen, and of the wives and children of wealthy Canadians. When the Canadian government decided to have a painting made of the Fathers of Confederation to celebrate the twentieth anniversary of the Confederation Conference, it selected Robert Harris as the artist.

Harris discovered that the job was more difficult than he had originally thought. Several "Fathers" had died, and the others were twenty years older than they had been in 1864. Robert had played in the orchestra for the Confederation Conference at Charlottetown, but that had been when he was only fifteen years old. Determined to be as accurate as possible, Harris sent questionnaires to people who had known the deceased politicians. He asked about the delegates' height, hair colour, whiskers, eyes, clothes, and even the size of their hands. Harris met with those Fathers of Confederation who were still living, and collected photographs of those who had died.

Self-portrait, Robert Harris
HC/CCAGM

The painting, which took Harris a year to finish, was completed in 1884 and brought him instant fame. It was hung in the Parliament Buildings at Ottawa. When the buildings were destroyed by fire in 1916, the painting was burned. By this time, Harris was sixty-seven years old, and his health and eyesight were poor. When he was asked to paint a replacement the best he could do was to let the government buy the charcoal sketch from which he had made the original *Fathers of Confederation* painting.

SPORTS

Organized sports on the Island owed much of their development in the late 1800s to the YMCA, the Caledonia Club and the Abegweit Athletic Club. The "Abbies" fielded teams in hockey, rugby, baseball, tennis, and track and field. Between 1900 and 1912, thanks largely to Bill Halpenny (Canadian pole-vault champion), James "Toby" MacMillan (Maritime sprint champion) and Michael Thomas (Maritime long-distance champion), the Abegweit Club won the Maritime track and field championship nine times.

Islanders love athletic competitions. The University of Prince Edward Island hockey, soccer and basketball teams receive extensive media and fan support. Recently, those teams have ranked among the best in Canada. Island hockey teams perform well in interprovincial competition, and Islanders keep close watch on the exploits of their National Hockey League stars. In recent times, Canada's smallest province has provided such NHL talents as Rick Vaive, Gerard Gallant, Forbes Kennedy, Allan MacAdam, Bob Stewart, Bobby and Billy MacMillan, Don Simmons, Errol Thompson and John Chabot. Youngsters do well nationally in such diverse sports as squash, racquetball, baseball and swimming.

Harness racing, however, has earned P.E.I. the title, "The Kentucky of Canada". Ths Island has more horses and more people involved in the horse industry per capita than any other province. Harness racing's roots go deep into the agricultural heritage of the Island. By the 1880s, over two dozen race tracks dotted the countryside. The introduction of night time parimutuel racing at the Charlottetown Driving Park in 1946, however, brought an end to many of the smaller Island tracks. Night racing meant that horse owners no longer had to take time off from work, and the general public could attend more easily. The crowning event of each year is the Gold Cup and Saucer Race, which is held during Old Home Week. Since 1961, the Gold Cup and Saucer Parade has added to the lustre of this season-ending event.

CHANGES IN ISLAND HARNESS RACING

1889	*first race in Charlottetown Driving Park*
1892	*pneumatic tires for sulkies*
1895	*drivers wear distinguishing caps and jackets*
1932	*horses classified by money winnings, rather than best time*
1938	*P.E.I. joins the United States Trotting Association for better rule enforcement*
1946	*mobile starting gate*
1947	*photo finish by high-speed movie camera*
1960	*Gold Cup and Saucer Race*
1981	*Saul's Pride runs first 2:00 mile*

THE BICYCLE CRAZE

The development of the modern bicycle in 1885, with its diamond-shaped frame, equal-sized wheels and endless chain, and the adoption of pneumatic tires three years later, began a bicycle craze in North America. The new cycle provided cheap transportation. Telegraph boys sped down the road to deliver messages. Doctors rode bicycles for house calls. Chaperones were amongst the first casualties, and waist-pinching corsets and multi-layered petticoats with their whalebone stiffeners were not far behind. Bicycle racing also became very popular on P.E.I.

THE GREAT ROAD RACE

A vast crowd, representing lovers of the wheel, lovers perhaps of the wheelmen, ladies and gentlemen of leisure and small boys, lined the St. Peter's Road last evening in one dense mass from the railway crossing to Brown's corner.

As usual, accidents were quite common. Mr. Moore collided with a cow, which injured the fork of his wheel and impeded his speed afterwards. Mr. Haszard was unfortunate to break his handle-bars before leaving and had to borrow one. Mr. Duchemin when coming down the first hill struck a stone and was thrown from his wheel and rendered unable to take any further active part in the race....

The first prize to Mr. Unsworth was a valuable bicycle lantern. The second prize to Mr. Morris was a pair of opera glasses, and Mr. Haszard won the cyclometer and bicycle bell.

Afterwards, there was an ice-cream and strawberry banquet, followed by speeches and a feast.

EIGHTEEN

> Working wives are a menace to the general welfare, to the public health and to the morals of the nation.
>
> A married woman's place is in the home...
>
> A married woman takes on a new name and new legal rights when she marries. She does not keep her identity as does a man...
>
> In being the superwomen they pretend, working wives cannot do two jobs well. They neglect either home or job. They cannot be dignified by the names of workers. They are chiselers, deserters from their post of duty, the home...
>
> Civilization can only advance when married women are protected in their natural career of homemaking.
>
> A married woman should be proud of giving herself to her home instead of priding herself on holding a job in a little office.
>
> *The Guardian, July 22, 1939*

THE STRUGGLE FOR WOMEN'S RIGHTS

"

Why can't women be ministers, Marilla? I asked Mrs. Lynde that and she was shocked and said it would be a scandalous thing.... She hoped that we never would. But I don't see why. I think women would make splendid ministers.... I'm sure Mrs. Lynde can pray every bit as well...and I've no doubt she could preach, too, with a little practice."

This statement was made by Anne Shirley, the heroine of Lucy Maud Montgomery's book, *Anne of Green Gables.* Many Island girls must have asked similar questions. In pioneer times, women and men worked side-by-side. It wasn't until 1836 that women couldn't vote. As the division of labour became more pronounced, men's and women's roles in society changed. During most of the 19th and early 20th centuries, women were not allowed to serve on juries. Females were not encouraged to go to school beyond the primary level, much less attend university. They were not permitted to become doctors or lawyers, nor allowed to vote, run for government or sit on schoolboards. According to the Election Act of the Dominion of Canada, an eligible voter in Canada was defined in 1890 as: *A male person, including an Indian, and excluding a person of Mongolian or Chinese race.... No woman, idiot, lunatic or criminal shall vote.*

Women were expected—and sometimes told—to quit their jobs when they married. A married woman had few rights. Her husband controlled the family's money, including any income earned by the wife. Fathers had sole legal control over the children. Women were thought to be capable of performing only a few jobs, and were con-

Acadian women at work
Media services, Halifax

sidered too weak, too emotional, and not intelligent enough to be politicians, business people, ministers, school principals and professionals. This severely limited their choices: they could marry and become housewives, or they could teach school, be maids, nurses, secretaries, store clerks, nuns or factory workers. Occupations such as nursing, dressmaking and public school teaching came to be thought of as "women's work".

Because women were limited in their choices by the written and unwritten laws made by men, they learned to function in other areas. They formed and managed charity organizations, Women's Institutes, and hospital and church auxiliary groups. Women raised funds through sales of baked goods, quilts and other handmade items to pay for the maps, globes, chalk and water buckets that were desperately needed by local schools. They looked after many of the details which held families and communities together. Women were closely in touch with the cycle of life—from midwifery to the preparation of the dead for burial.

Many women became involved in missionary organizations, for which they organized fund-raising drives and served as missionaries in foreign fields. In 1884, for example, the Women's Baptist Missionary Union of the Maritime Provinces had twelve branches in P.E.I., and Bay View sisters Martha and Dr. Zella Clark performed heroic work as missionaries/doctors in China at the turn of the 20th century.

Although women often did exactly the same type of work as men, they were paid less money than were the men. This was just as true for the women who worked in lobster canneries as it was for teachers. Even in "women's jobs", workers were strictly controlled. In some factories, female workers were not allowed to mix with male workers. Factory owners told female workers what to wear and how to cut their hair.

THE RIGHT TO VOTE

In 1916, an important event occurred in the history of Prince Edward Island. The Women's Liberal Club was formed under Margaret Rogers Stewart and Elsie Inman. Stewart and Inman and eighty-eight other women decided it was time Island women had the right to vote. The Women's Liberal Club wrote for advice to *suffragettes* such as Nellie McClung and Emily Murphy who were leading the fight for the vote and equal status of women in Manitoba and Alber-

WOMEN WIN THE RIGHT TO VOTE

Manitoba	1916
Saskatchewan	1916
Alberta	1916
British Columbia	1917
Ontario	1917
Nova Scotia	1918
New Brunswick	1919
P.E.I.	1922
Newfoundland	1925
Quebec	1940

ta. They decided that the best way to accomplish their goal was to convert men to their views. In a quiet way, this group of determined women began to change old ideas about women's place in society. They spoke about women's rights and needs to various groups across the Island, to members of government, and to all the women they met.

The first major breakthrough in women's battle to gain the right to vote came during the First World War. Many women took over jobs left by the men who went overseas to fight. They became involved in the Red Cross and in making clothes for the soldiers. They worked on assembly lines in factories, dressed in overalls and trousers. They did "men's work", and did it well. Partly as a result of this success, but more for political reasons, women who had relatives in the army were allowed to vote in the 1917 Canadian election. The next year, all women over the age of twenty-one received the right to vote in federal elections.

Unlike the situation in other provinces, Island women made few attempts to gain the franchise prior to the war. When John Dewar proposed such a measure in the legislature in 1918, the male politicians decided to wait until the women demanded the right to vote in provincial elections. The *Charlottetown Examiner*, however, declared: "Can women perform aright the multifarious duties of the home, follow the fashions closely, give time to social matters, take a lively interest in current news and gossip, etc., and also attend closely to matters and questions of political importance?"

The Women's Liberal Club knew they could, and began to actively lobby the members of the legislature and recruit help from the Women's Institutes, which had been formed in 1913. In response to several petitions in 1922, Premier John Bell announced that Island women should have the franchise because they voted in federal elections, they had helped win the war, it would help to broaden women's "subjects of conversation and study", and the public would benefit from their advice on matters of morals, health and the family. Despite one member's complaint that a woman's "place is in the home, in the kitchen looking after home affairs", Island women received the franchise in 1922.

Not everyone was happy with this decision—especially some men. Senator Elsie Inman described the problems some women had at this time.

■

Most of the women were afraid of their husbands. The majority of husbands refused to let them vote. Well, I remember taking a woman—she said she'd vote, but she was scared to vote because her husband threatened her if he saw her at a poll. She was anxious to vote and I said, "Would he know you if you were dressed up in other clothes?" Well, she didn't think he would, so I went home and she was about my size. We wore veils in those days, so I took my clothes and coat and put the veil on her and took her to vote....

I went to the door to get another woman to vote and her husband met me and said, "Get out of this, trying to lead my wife astray, you should be ashamed of this. You're from a nice family, and have a good husband, you should be ashamed of yourself."

WOMEN TODAY

Gradually, women have been gaining equality with men in other areas than the right to vote. In 1965 in Prince Edward Island, women gained the privilege to sit on juries. Nine years later, the minimum wage was equalized for males and females. In 1977, the federal government passed a law to make it an offence to discriminate against women. More and more women are employed in what are called "non-traditional" jobs. In 1983 Leone Bagnall became the Minister of Education, and Marian Reid was made Speaker of the House in the 1980s. There are increasing numbers of women practicing medicine and law, and more women in business, or doing carpentry, truck driving and other work which traditionally had been done solely by men.

Today, women still face discrimination. Top business and professional jobs continue to be more difficult for women to obtain. Females are still expected to take "women's jobs", and are often paid less money than men for doing equal work. Although there have been many changes in the last hundred years in the way women are treated in society, there are still many injustices. These include continuing discrimination by employers based on gender and marital status, sexual harassment in the workplace, rape, battered women, insufficient daycare facilities, and inadequate maternity leave privileges. Pension plans often leave women, whose husbands predecease them, with meagre funds upon which to exist. And senior citizens, the majority of whom are elderly women, require greater support.

MONA WILSON

Mona Wilson was the most important individual in the development of public health on Prince Edward Island. In 1923, when she began her work on the Island as a Red Cross nurse, few people knew about proper nutrition and health care. Most children had at least one physical defect. She helped form Junior Red Cross clubs which instructed club members on the importance of bathing once or twice a week, leaving a bedroom window open at night, and eating fresh vegetables, fruit, and whole wheat bread. The basic rural diet consisted of pork, salt cod, potatoes, turnips, pie and plenty of sweets. Milk was saved for the pigs and foxes. Everyone, including children, drank tea.

Finally, in 1931, the Island government set up a Department of Health, and Red Cross nurses, employed by the government and supervised by Mona Wilson, were able to make greater improvements in public health.

NINETEEN

Debki Dancers, from A STREAM OUT OF LEBANON,
Institute of Island Studies, 1988

A MULTICULTURAL ISLAND

Although the Island is the most culturally homogeneous Canadian province, over sixty different nationalities are represented on Prince Edward Island. The Micmac arrived about two thousand years ago, followed by the Acadians in the early 18th century, and then by English, Scottish and Irish settlers in the late 18th and 19th centuries. By 1861, the population had grown to about eighty thousand. Most of the other ethnic groups in P.E.I. immigrated to the Island since the Second World War. Significantly, it was not until 1975 that the first non-British mayor of Charlottetown (Frank Zakem) was elected.

A small German settlement apparently existed briefly on the Island in the Acadian period, but it was not until the Loyalists arrived following the American Revolution that P.E.I. had a permanent German population. Today, the German population is spread from Cape Kildare to Souris, and they are integrated into the society around them. To avoid discrimination, many early German settlers anglicized their names—Henckells became Jenkins, Eichorns became Acorns, and Junkers became Younkers.

Another non-British, non-French ethnic group which came to the Island was the Lebanese. In the late 1800s, the Christian Lebanese were experiencing persecution under the Turks. Many Lebanese heard about North America and decided they could create a better life for themselves in the "New World". In some cases, families and even whole villages emigrated to America. Many people from Lebanon went to the United States, but a small group settled in Canada. The first Lebanese settlers arrived in Prince Edward Island in the 1880s. Many of the young Lebanese men established themselves as "pack pedlars". These merchants travelled from farm to farm on foot, by train, or by horse and wagon, selling everything from tea to trousers. They provided a needed service for many farming families who seldom got to town. Although the farmers were at first wary of the strangers, they soon began to look forward to the pedlars' visits, and offered food and lodging to them when they came. Through hard work, many of the merchants earned enough money to open small stores, some of which still exist today. The Lebanese have done well, and Islanders elected the first premier of Lebanese origin in Canada (Joe Ghiz).

PRINCE EDWARD ISLAND

POPULATION

ETHNIC ORIGINS, 1986

British	86,410
British and French	15,180
French	11,130
British and other	5,985
Dutch	1,280
German	535
French and other	420
Native Peoples	410
Lebanese	230
South Asian	205
Scandinavian	135
Chinese	130
Polish	100

TOTAL POPULATION 125,090

Data from Canada Year Book, 1990 (estimated)

ACADIAN CULTURE: THE STRUGGLE TO SURVIVE

Prior to 1860, Acadians lived in their own communities and generally avoided contact with English-speaking settlers. One reason for this was their desire to keep their Acadian culture and traditions. Since Acadian school children were instructed almost solely in French, most Acadians could not speak English. In the 1860s and 1870s, the provincial government ordered Acadian schools to teach every subject (except French) in the English language. Acadian teachers and Roman Catholic priests, such as Georges-Antoine Belcourt, fought against this attempt to destroy Acadian culture.

FATHER GEORGES-ANTOINE BELCOURT

In the fall of 1859, a French-speaking priest from Lower Canada arrived on the Island to become pastor of Rustico. He came at the request of the bishop who was short of priests to serve Acadian parishes. Father Belcourt, then fifty-six years old, had worked for twenty-eight years as a missionary among the Indians and Metis in Manitoba and Minnesota. Upon arriving in Rustico, Father Belcourt immediately set to work to improve the Acadians' quality of life. Island Acadians were generally very poor, had small farms and were in debt to the landlords. Father Belcourt first established the Catholic Institute of Rustico (a temperance society for men), through which he started many worthwhile projects.

The Institute met regularly to hear lectures on economics, farming, science and geography. One of the projects introduced by Belcourt was the creation of the Farmers' Bank of Rustico, the forerunner of the Credit Union movement in North America. It was the smallest chartered bank in Canada. The basis of the Rustico Bank was co-operation. Belcourt thought that by running their own bank, Acadian farmers would learn about economics, and could borrow money more cheaply than they could elsewhere. It would also allow them to get loans for seed grain, additional farmland, and help maintain a spirit of independence in Acadian communities. Another of Belcourt's ideas was to find farmland for the younger generation. He supervised an "out-migration" project which sent a few hundred Acadians from the Island to settle in Lower Canada and New Brunswick. Today, many of the descendants of Island Acadians live in Quebec and New Brunswick.

Father Belcourt also wanted to train bilingual teachers, and thus help preserve the French language and Acadian culture. To achieve this, he established a French High School which he operated for a few years until a sufficient number of good teachers were available. He also created a library with a good selection of French books. Members of the Institute raised money for these projects by holding large "tea parties". Donations were also received from friends in Lower Canada and France, and even from Napoleon III, the Emperor of France.

ACADIAN CULTURAL NATIONALISM

The rise of a sense of Acadian nationalism throughout the Maritimes helped Island Acadians in their struggle to preserve their own culture. In 1864, an Acadian college was built in New Brunswick, and a French newspaper, *Le Moniteur Acadien*, began in 1867. In the next several years, other French-language newspapers were started, including *l'Impartial* (1893–1915) in Tignish. The Acadian Teachers' Association, a home and school association, and the Saint Thomas Aquinas Society were created to promote French-language education. Maritime Acadians also met in large conventions to discuss their problems and to find ways to preserve their culture. An Acadian flag, anthem, a patron saint and an official feast day resulted from these conventions.

Without government assistance, without French-speaking teachers and without money, the Acadian leaders fought an uphill battle. Many Acadian children were forced to attend English-speaking classes. By 1966, only one-half of all Acadian people could read or understand French. In the 1960s, however, the Island government changed its educational policies. It decided that in districts with a large number of Acadians, classes could be taught in French. The first such area was Evangeline. Today, Acadian art and culture are experiencing a rebirth.

The Acadian Flag

THE OLDEST ISLANDERS

The Micmac had even more problems than the Acadians in maintaining their culture. After the conquest, the British government was not as friendly towards the Micmac as France had been. Following the peace treaty of 1763, the British gave small amounts of land to the Micmac in New Brunswick and Nova Scotia. However, on Prince Edward Island all the land—which once had belonged to the Micmac—was given away by lottery to wealthy Brits.

To most British settlers and administrators, the Micmac were an invisible people. After two years of gathering information about the

Island, Governor Walter Patterson reported in 1772 that there were "no Natives, or Indians, who either inhabit, or claim any right to" P.E.I. Since the number of Micmac was so small, and no treaty had been negotiated with them, the government could safely ignore their presence. When the British settlers thought of the natives, they were quite willing to see them pass out of existence, "like leaves before the autumn's blast."

For a while, the Micmac continued to roam the Island in search of game. As the number of European settlers increased, they cleared the forests and erected fences, and killed the wild animals. The Micmac were no longer able to move their camps freely from place to place. They asked the government for land of their own, but the government was unwilling to help the Micmac. Finally, Sir James Montgomery, a wealthy British landlord, offered to let the Micmac live on Lennox Island rent-free.

The government thought that Lennox Island was a perfect spot. It would separate the Micmac from the settlers and prevent trouble. The Micmac would also be able to live as they wished. A Catholic missionary, Abbé de Callone, persuaded several Micmac families to settle year-round on Lennox Island, where they built a chapel, cleared several hectares of land and planted potatoes. Unfortunately, the land was not very fertile, as one-third of Lennox Island was swampy. Moreover, settlers came to Lennox Island to cut the wild hay in the marshes to feed their livestock. Despite Micmac complaints, the marshland was rented to the settlers rather than to the Indians who could not pay for it. The Micmac asked the government to buy Lennox Island for them, but nothing was done.

In addition to the work of Abbé de Callone, Thomas Irwin sought to provide education for the Micmac, and Baptist missionary Silas Rand lobbied the government to meet the natives' spiritual and physical needs. No one, however, laboured harder to ensure Micmac survival than Indian commissioner Theophilus Stewart.

By the 1830s, no one was sure how many Micmac were living on the Island. Guesses ranged from two hundred to five hundred. It was difficult to determine the exact number because very few remained in the same location for very long. Hunting and fishing required them to move from place to place. Only a handful of families lived year-round on Lennox Island, although large numbers gathered there in July to celebrate Saint Anne's Day. Favourite camping grounds included Crapaud, Egmont Bay, Indian River, Morell, St. Peter's, and near the Charlottetown harbour. In addition to

TO THE GREAT LEADERS OF PRINCE EDWARD ISLAND

Fathers, — Before the white men crossed the great waters — our woods offered us food and clothes in plenty — the waters gave us fish — and the woods game — our fathers were hardy, brave and free — we knew no want — we were the only owners of the land.

Fathers, — When the French came to us they asked us for land to set up their wigwams — we gave it freely — In return they taught us new arts — protected and cherished us — sent holy men who taught us Christianity — who made books for us — and taught us to read them — that was good — and we were grateful.

Fathers, — When your fathers came and drove away our French fathers — we were left alone, — our people were sorry, but they were brave — they raised the war cry — and took up the tomahawk against your fathers. — Then your fathers spoke to us — and said, put up the axe — we will protect you — we will become your fathers. — Our fathers and your fathers had long talks around the council fire — the hatchets were buried — and we became friends.

Fathers, — They promised to leave us some of our land — but they did not — They drove us from place to place like wild beasts — that was not just.

Fathers, — Our tribe in Nova Scotia, Canada, New Brunswick and Cape Breton, have land on which their families are happy. — We ask of you, Fathers, to give us a part of the land that was once our fathers' — where we may raise our wigwams without disturbance — and plough and sow — that we may live, and our children also — else, Fathers, you may soon see not one drop of Indian blood in this Island. Where is our land? — we have none. —

Fathers, we are poor — do not forget us — remember the promises your fathers made to ours. Fathers, we salute you.

(Signed) Louis Francouis Alguimou,
Piel Jaques,
Oliver Thoma,
Peter Tony,
Micael Michell.

hunting and fishing, the Micmac supplemented their income by selling firewood, woodsplint baskets and birchbark goods. The men fashioned barrels, furniture, ship fittings, brooms, axe handles, toy bows and arrows, snowshoes and canoes. The women made beautiful beaded cloth goods, boxes with porcupine quillwork mosaics, and birchbark utensils embroidered with animal hair. Woodsplint baskets, made by the whole family, were the most popular items. When all else failed, the Micmac were forced to beg for food and clothing.

The Micmac asked the government for land, food or money in return for the land that had been taken from them. An edited copy of the petition they sent to the government of Prince Edward Island in 1832 reads as follows:

There were several attempts to provide land for the Micmac. Charles Worrell, a wealthy landowner, gave property to six Micmac families. However, after making improvements to the land, the natives were forced off it by Irish settlers. Ten acres were loaned to the

Micmac celebrate the St. Anne's Day Festival
with traditional clothing and song.
The Guardian

Micmac on the east side of Charlottetown harbour, but their white neighbours refused to allow the Micmac to cross their land. Then, in 1866, the government built a hospital on this Micmac property.

In the early 1840s, the government finally acknowledged the Micmac's plight by granting pauper relief to several poverty-stricken natives. As Governor Fitzroy wrote in 1840: "With few exceptions, they are sunk to the most abject and degraded state to which I should conceive it possible for human beings to arrive." In the mid-1850s, the government appointed two Indian commissioners (Theophilus Stewart and Henry Palmer) to encourage the Micmac to engage in farming and thus become self-sufficient, and granted them a small budget to care for the Micmac's needs. In 1865, Stewart attended the annual meeting of the Aborigines Protection Society in London, England. Although this society was dedicated to helping native groups around the world, it had generally ignored the Maritime Indians. Stewart's visit changed its priorities. Five years later, the Aborigines Protection Society purchased Lennox Island for the Micmac and helped them survey the land and build roads.

When P.E.I. entered Confederation in 1873, the Micmac came under the control of the federal government. At this time, the Micmac culture was in a sad state. The only school set aside for the natives refused to teach the Micmac language. The Island government sometimes gave the Micmac bread, tea, flour, pork, blankets and medicine, but they could not count on receiving these supplies. If the Micmac were not able to sell their baskets and other wares, they starved. The Canadian government was not very concerned about the Micmac. By 1880, the native population had fallen to 266 and it appeared that the Micmac might disappear from the Island. But the Micmac refused to die. They hunted geese in the spring, fished and dug shellfish in the summer, and made axe handles, baskets and oars in the winter to sell to nearby farms. By 1917 there were reserves at Lennox Island, Morell, Scotchfort and Rocky Point.

A large number of Micmac volunteered for service during the two World Wars, or worked in war-related industries. Gradually, more and more natives discarded their traditional clothing and adopted the values and lifestyles of the white society. In the late 1940s, the federal government coerced the Micmac into living on Lennox Island by providing social assistance only to those who resided on this reserve. Lennox Island had its own elementary school, but older students had to attend a residential high school in Schubenacadie,

Nova Scotia. Here, Micmac children were separated from their parents for the school year, and all instruction was in English.

The Micmac were denied the right to vote (unless they were war veterans), were prohibited from drinking alcohol, and were not legally considered citizens until 1957. Until recently, Indian women who married non-Natives lost their Indian status (as did their offspring). Non-status Micmac now outnumber status Micmac on the Island.

Perhaps the most important event in recent Micmac history came in 1973 when the government built a causeway between Lennox Island and P.E.I. No longer isolated, and given more freedom to administer its affairs, the Lennox Island Band began to provide for itself. It started an oyster co-op in 1972, followed by peat moss, handicrafts and blueberry industries. In 1972, the Morell, Scotchfort and Rocky Point reserves formed the Abegweit Band, and embarked on their own economic projects. The Micmac language is now taught in the Lennox Island school, and the natives are actively attempting to preserve their traditions.

When asked what the Micmac want, John Joe Sark of Lennox Island replied in 1987 that they "are looking for basically the same things all of us are looking for. First of all, to be put on an equal footing with you. We do a little of everything now, but we do not have sufficient land base or resources.... We have to have our own type of government. We are sophisticated enough to find solutions to our own problems. Our future lies with developing along with our neighbours around us, being allowed to change that lifestyle at our own speed."

TWENTY

Horse-drawn scoops are used to gather Irish Moss along the shore after a summer storm.
PEIDOT

THE ISLAND WAY

F or the last several decades, Prince Edward Island has been trying to decide where its destiny lies. Some Islanders point to the Island's high unemployment rate, and an average income that falls well below the national level, to support their demands that P.E.I. adopt all the latest technological and economic advances. Other people wish to return to past values, and worry that the Island is losing its separate identity and endangering its environment by adopting non-Island ways. Although these conflicting views of the future are present almost everywhere, they can best be seen in regard to tourism, land use and the fixed link.

TOURISM

Since the 1880s there has been a concerted effort to develop P.E.I. as a tourist mecca based upon its natural beaches, lush rolling countryside, congeniality and cultural heritage. Although tourism provides many jobs and has become the province's most important industry, not everyone has been happy with its growth. Ever since the 1908 debate about allowing automobiles on the roads, Islanders have agonized over how much to cater to visitors at the expense of traditional customs. The tourist literature emphasizes P.E.I.'s pastoral nature, and offers an escape from the cares of city life. Yet, as more and more tourists travel to the Island (over 700,000 in 1989), traffic jams, parking problems, air pollution and petty crime tend to destroy this idllyic environment. As the number of tourists increases, the unspoiled landscape is despoiled. Precious sand dunes are destroyed, cottages border the shoreline where farms once stood, commercial strips detract from the picturesque scenery, and roadside signs advertise water slides and miniature castles.

The ensuing conflict between modernization and traditional values typifies the pull between old and new. In 1974, Kings County successfully opposed the creation of a National Park in the eastern end of the county. The Land Use Commission has several times refused to allow commercial development on prime agricultural land. At other times, however, the jobs created by golf courses, theme parks and water slides have carried the day.

Much of this debate rests on some residents' conviction that the Island's economy and values rest with the rural independent farmer. In reality, however, the size of Island farms has steadily in-

HEALTH CARE, 1987

TOTAL POPULATION PER:

	PHYSICIAN	DENTIST	OPTO-METRIST	NURSE	PHARMA-CIST
P.E.I.	696	2,512	15,850	111	1,884
N.S.	461	2,220	15,659	99	1,410
ONT.	433	1,705	11,492	97	1,836
CANADA	467	1,910	10,308	107	1,578

Source: Canada Year Book, *1990*

ISLAND DIVORCES AND BIRTHS

YEARS	AVERAGE DIVORCES	BIRTHS PER 1,000 PEOPLE
1941–45	2	23.7
1946–50	21	30.5
1951–55	10	27.2
1956–60	4	26.6
1960–65	8	25.7
1966–70	45	18.9
1971–75	70	17.3
1976–80	139	16.1
1981–85	208	15.6
1987	812	14.9

creased throughout this century, while the number of farmers has declined. Crop specialization, and the rise of such large marketing and processing firms as Cavendish Farms, has eroded the farmers' independence. Concerned with the decline of the rural family farm and with the threat to the environment, several Island historians and their supporters have sought to return P.E.I. to its "golden age" in the 1860s, when the people supposedly valued conservation, self-reliance, community and the family farm. The 1979 temporary ban on new shopping malls, which were threatening to undermine the traditional country store, revealed the pastoral appeal of their ideas. Their failure to prevent school consolidation, which they believed would seriously undermine smaller rural communities, however, illustrated the allure of modernization.

The question of land use also reveals the pull between the desire for a better material life and the quiet rustic life of the countryside.

In the early 1970s, fears that prime agricultural land was falling under the control of "people from away" reawakened old memories of absentee landlords. In 1972, despite counter-arguments that individuals should be free to dispose of their land to the highest bidder, government legislation required non-residents to gain cabinet approval for sales of land exceeding ten acres, or 330 feet of shorefront property.

More recently, concerned groups have lobbied for effective legislation to prevent agricultural land from being acquired by large corporations. "The greatest threat to the family farm and to rural communities," declared the National Farmers Union, "is the encroachment into the field of farm production by industrial corporations." The government responded in 1982 by limiting corporate landholdings to three thousand acres. However, it set no limit upon how many acres a firm could lease.

Early in 1990, the P.E.I. government signed agreements with McCain Foods and Irving-owned Cavendish Farms to build two potato processing plants. When completed, these establishments will employ approximately three hundred people, and will result in forty per cent (rather than eighteen per cent) of the Island's potato crop being processed on P.E.I.. Once again, however, conservative and liberal beliefs clashed over the benefits of these changes. The processing plants' supporters revelled in the attention of such large companies, and at the reception held for the McCain Foods' announcement at the CP Prince Edward Hotel, the guests dined on smoked salmon and shrimp impaled on watermelon. *The Guardian* editorialized:

> *This is news almost too good to comprehend...after decades of shipping mainly raw produce and watching other provinces and countries process and profit from the added value, Prince Edward Island can smile— finally—at future prospects for the industry.*

Urban Laughlin, district director of the National Farmers Union, however, avoided the "carnival" atmosphere of the signing and spoke of the threat it posed to Island farmers, and questioned the government's commitment to the family farm. He called for anti-vertical integration laws, and demanded that the government concern itself with the growing disintegration of Island topsoil.

SMALL IS BEAUTIFUL

Two other examples of the Island's caution in accepting "modern" solutions are the province's rejection of Litton Industries and nuclear power. When the federal government granted a contract to Litton Systems of Canada to build a low-level air-defence system in 1985, it stipulated that the company construct some of the components in the Maritimes. After a short bidding war among the three provinces, P.E.I. was victorious. By now, however, concerned citizens had begun to protest the government's decision. Anti-war and anti-nuclear activists combined with traditionalists to demand changes in the agreement.

Janet Norgrove of New Glasgow, for example, wrote: "Primary production industries offer both economic and spiritual rewards to our communities and ourselves...farming provides a solid economic base for an entire community to build and grow upon. But what values do companies such as Litton offer? The value of profits before people, of war before peace, of death before life." A new government in 1986 had second thoughts. When Litton balked at making any long-term commitments, the Liberal Ghiz government cancelled the deal. "The government wants jobs for Islanders, but not at any price," Ghiz declared. "P.E.I. is not a banana republic." Anti-nuclear arguments and the "small is beautiful" approach had turned the tide.

Because Prince Edward Island possesses no coal, oil or hydro-electric power, it pays one of the highest prices for electrical power in Canada. The dramatic rise in world oil prices in 1973 served to highlight the province's economic disadvantage. When New Brunswick offered the Island part-ownership in 1977 in the construction of a CANDU nuclear power plant at Point Lepreau, it seemed a perfect opportunity to acquire reasonable electricity rates. The offer, however, sparked a heated controversy, and helped overturn the provincial government. Those people who favoured lower costs for electrical power, and a secure supply of power, opposed environmental groups that feared a nuclear catastrophe and argued for the development of wood, wind and water power. The end result was a decision to buy power from New Brunswick, but not to become a part-owner of the Point Lepreau nuclear plant.

FIXED LINK

The recent fixed-link plebiscite has also forced Islanders to think about their future. Since a fixed link would affect agriculture (cheaper transportation), fishing (possible environmental damages) and tourism (easier access), the issue has aroused intense controversy. Although much of the debate has focussed on economic matters, a major difference was each side's view of "progress". The slogans of the two opposing groups illustrated their priorities leading into the 1989 plebiscite. The pro-link platform was "Islanders for a Better Tomorrow", whereas the anti-link people called themselves "Friends of the Island". Proponents of a stronger economy and a better materialistic lifestyle conflicted with defenders of the environment and the "Island way of life".

The Northumberland Strait has usually been more of a psychological than a physical buffer. According to such people as Professor David Weale of the University of Prince Edward Island, loss of this insularity would trade the province's identity for an uncertain future. "The problem of low incomes and high unemployment which we share with the entire Atlantic region had nothing to do with our insularity," he wrote in 1988. "We offer some contrast to the boring, commercial, mass culture of North America. We also have a place to live that is wonderfully free from congestion and pollution." Although sixty per cent of the people voted in favour of a fixed link, environmental concerns threaten to postpone construction indefinitely.

Despite attempts to resist change, P.E.I. has not been immune to the influences of the outside world. In fact, many of the people who trumpet the benefits of traditionalism come "from away". Having experienced life elsewhere, they chose to remain on P.E.I., and now struggle vigorously to protect its way of life. However, it should be remembered that only ten per cent of the population is actively engaged in agriculture, and that tourism ranks either first or second in generating provincial income.

Civil service jobs provide incomes for a larger proportion of the population than in any other province (approximately nine thousand jobs), and the provincial government relies on its federal counterpart for over one-half of its revenues. Although the Island might seem over-governed for a province of only 127,000 people, it possesses a sort of direct democracy. Each elected member to the provincial government, for example, represents about four thousand citizens. In Ontario, by contrast, each provincial member serves over seventy thousand people. The people know and have access to their elected representatives. The resulting feeling that they can affect government policies explains why Prince Edward Island usually has the highest voting turnout ratio in Canada. Perhaps the Island way of life is worth the struggle.

APPENDIX

LEARNING MORE

The writing of this book suffered from having both too much and too little information. Such Island topics as Confederation, the absentee landlords, and the writings of Lucy Maud Montgomery have been explored elsewhere in considerable detail. To summarize them in a relatively few pages, however, seems an injustice. Prince Edward Island is also rich in community histories. Indeed, several of these books, which examine only one lot or village, equal or exceed the length of this study, which surveys the Island's entire lifespan from pre-history to the present. The problem of deciding what to exclude was thus a challenging task. Certainly, no one will agree with all my selections.

For those people who wish to learn more, I suggest the following sources. For the early history of the Acadians, see D.C. Harvey, *The French Regime in Prince Edward Island*, and for their subsequent history consult Georges Arsenault, *The Island Acadians, 1720-1980*. For general studies on the pre-Confederation and Confederation periods read F.W.P. Bolger (ed.), *Canada's Smallest Province*, and David Weale and Harry Baglole, *The Island and Confederation: The End of an Era*. *The Garden Transformed*, edited by Verner Smitheram (et al.) examines selected topics from 1945 to 1980. Wayne MacKinnon, *The Life of the Party*, chronicles the history of the Liberal Party; and Kennedy Wells, *The Fishery of Prince Edward Island*, outlines the fishing industry from the early Micmac period to the present. The only books that attempt to survey the sweep of Island history are A.H. Clark, *Three Centuries and the Island* (1959); Bolger, *Canada's Smallest Province* (1973); and Errol Sharpe, *A People's History of Prince Edward Island* (1976). Pre-twentieth-century Islanders are provided excellent coverage in the multiple volumes of *The Dictionary of Canadian Biography*. The most readable and eclectic source is *The Island Magazine*, which has been published twice yearly since 1976.

Many aspects of Island history, however, have been largely ignored. Other than the Acadians and the Lebanese, ethnic groups have been overlooked. There are several studies on the Roman Catholic Church, but no comprehensive account of the various Protestant denominations. The impact of the two World Wars and the Great Depression has been ignored, as have such topics as temperance, 20th-century urban history, the economy, labour, the family, social services and crime. Biography, usually one of the most popular forms of historical writing, has been generally absent from Island studies. The 20th century has been particularly overlooked. A crucial absence is the want of research on the role of women in Island society. The research materials are not lacking, but the writers are. I suspect that the absence of a graduate program at the University of Prince Edward Island has led many researchers to pursue non-Island topics upon continuing their studies at off-Island universities. Unaware of the richness of the primary documents on P.E.I., graduate advisors tend to steer their students to other topics. Only U.P.E.I. offers a course on Island history, and few universities outside the Maritimes provide courses on the region. I know of one history professor in Alberta who informs his first-year students that P.E.I. only deserves one lecture per year.

GENEALOGY

Genealogy is the third most popular hobby in North America, behind coin and stamp collecting. In the summers, especially, the Provincial Archives and the Prince Edward Island Museum and Heritage Foundation cater to hundreds of people interested in tracing their family trees. Novice genealogists would benefit from the experience of these two organizations in their research of Island connections.

INDEX

L

Land
auction, 79
Land Purchase Act, 91
  1853, 89
Land Use Commission, 174, 176
Laughlin, Urban, 176, 178
Lawrence, Charles, 46
Laws
  early, 77
Lawson, David, 55
Lebanese, 181, 184
Liberal
  government, 177, 179
  party, 181, 184
Linkletter, John, 110
Litton, 177, 179
Lobster, 14, 108, 109
London Conference, 96
Longfellow, Henry, 47
Lot 31, 54
Lot 33, 54
Lot 36, 56, 57
Lot 40, 54
Lot 56
  murder at Bay Fortune, 84
Lot 59, 54
Lottery, 53
Louisbourg, 33, 37, 38, 46, 47, 52
Louisiana, 59
Loyalists, 55, 67, 78
Lumbering, 97

M

M. Butcher Market, 74
MacDonald, A.A., 96
MacDonald, Captain John, 54, 56

Macdonald, John A., 94, 95, 99
MacEachern, Angus Bernard, 72
Mackinnon, John L., 110
MacKinnon, Wayne, 181, 184
Magdalen Islands, 52, 72
Malpeque, 33, 37, 49, 54
Manitoba
  confederation, 96
  women's rights, 158, 160
Maritime Union, 94
  Charlottetown meeting, 95
Marketing
  fish, 109
Maynard, Will, 114
McCain Foods, 176, 178
McClung, Nellie, 158, 160
McDonald, Donald (1783-1867), 71
McGee, D'Arcy, 95
McLeod, Malcolm, 110
  mice, 36, 38
Micmac, 37, 40, 65
  and alcohol, 43
  disease, 42
  handicrafts, 42
  religious beliefs, 43
  shamans, 43
  wigwams, 41
Mill, 110
Mill River, 14
Minegoo, 81
  See also Micmac
Mink, 114
Miscouche, 66
Mont Carmel, 66
Montague River, 34
Montgomery, Lucy Maud, 12, 181, 184
  Anne of Green Gables, 157, 159
Montgomery, Sir James, 54, 55, 57
Mud diggers, 109, 110
Murphy, Emily, 158, 160
Muskrat, 114
Mussel mud, 109, 110

N

O

P

Processing
   fish, 109
Property qualification, 76
Protestant, 181, 184
   Scottish, 78
Province House, 93, 95
Provincial government, 178,
180

Q

Quebec, 53
   confederation, 94
Quebec City, 95
Quebec Conference, 95, 96
Queens County, 53
Queen Victoria, The
   Charlottetown Conference, 95
Quit rent, 54, 78

R

Railway, 99
Rayner, B.I., 113
Rayner, Silas, 113
Red Cross, 159, 161
   Mona Wilson, 161
Reid, Marian, 160, 162
Religion, 71
   missionaries, 43
   priests, 40, 43, 46
Rent, 86, 87
Responsible government, 88, 89
   Prince Edward Island, 1851,
   89
Revenue, 178, 180
Richards, William
   shipbuilder, 102
Rocky Point, 52
Rogers, David, 110
Rollo Bay, 66
Rollo, Lord, 46, 49, 52

Roma, Jean Pierre, 34
Roman Catholic, 33, 54, 66, 67,
72
   Church, 181, 184
   Irish, 78
   missionaries, 41
   Scottish Catholics, 55
Round Market, 74

S

Saint Anne's Day, 41
Saint Pierre, Comte de, 33
Saskatchewan
   confederation, 96
Savage Harbour, 33
School, 158, 159
   consolidation, 175, 177
Schurman, M.S., 110
Scotchfort, 57
Scots
   Gaelic, 67
   Highlanders, 67
   Scottish Catholics, 55
   Scottish Protestants, 55
Scurvy, 40
Second World War, 181, 184
Selkirk
   land purchase, 89
Senate, 96
Settlers, 34
   English, 67
Sharpe, Errol, 181, 184
Shellfish, 109
Shipbuilding, 97, 102
Shipyard
   Grand River, 102
   Mount Stewart, 102
   New Glasgow, 102
   Port Hill, 102
   Souris, 102
Silver fox, 114
Size, 13

Y

P rofessor Douglas Baldwin came "from away" to teach history at the University of Prince Edward Island from 1979 through 1986. During that period, the Toronto-born historian pursued exhaustive research into the facts and folklore that shape the history of Canada's smallest province. He has written books and scholarly articles on many facets of Island life, from financial institutions to public health, and has lectured throughout Canada, Great Britain and the United States.

Land of the Red Soil—his eighth book—is the first comprehensive popular history of Prince Edward Island. In addition to *Abegweit, Land of the Red Soil*, the social studies text that precedes this updated and revised work, Douglas Baldwin is co-editor of *Gaslights, Epidemics and Vagabond Cows: Charlottetown in the Victorian Era* (Ragweed Press, 1988).

He now teaches in the history department at Acadia University in Nova Scotia; and is writing the biography of Red Cross nurse Mona Gordon Wilson (1894–1981), the principal architect of public health services on Prince Edward Island.